WE WILL STAND

The Real Story

Behind The Songs, Artists & Executives That Built The Contemporary Christian Music Industry

STAN MOSER

Christian Music United, 419 Dahlia Dr. Brentwood, TN 37027.

All pictures used by permission as noted throughout the book.
Pictures shown at the beginning of each section:
Blowing In The Wind (pages 12-13)
- Andrae Crouch—© CCMMagazine.com
- Larry Norman—© CCMMagazine.com
- Evie—© Word Music Entertainment
- Pastor Chuck Smith—© The Book of Love Song
- Love Song (Bob Wall, Tommy Coomes, John Mehler, Chuck Girard, Jay Truax)—© The Book of Love Song
- Barry McGuire—© CCMMagazine.com
- Phil Keaggy—© Word Music Entertainment

CCM UNITED
ONE MESSAGE. MANY VOICES.

The Times They Are A Changin' (pages 58-59)
Chris Christian, White Heart & Dick Clark—© YMCLLC Productions
Keith Green—© CCMMagazine.com
Michael Omartian—© CCMMagazine.com
Petra (John Lawry, Bob Hartman, Louie Weaver, Mark Kelly, John Schlitt)—© Word Music Entertainment
Steve Green—© CCMMagazine.com

Gotta Serve Somebody (pages 150-151)
Rich Mullins—© CCMMagazine.com
Rebecca St. James—© CCMMagazine.com
Michael English—© Word Music Entertainment
Steven Curtis Chapman, Twila Paris—© Capitol Christian Music Group
Carman—© CCM Magazine.com
4HIM (Andy Chrisman, Mark Harris, Marty Magehee & Kirk Sullivan)—© CCMMagazine.com

Cover design and layout, Beverly Wallbrech (Subtlemonsters.com)

Editorial support, Ed Chinn (CoolRiverPub.com)

Printed in the Unites States of America

CCMUnited.com

TABLE OF CONTENTS

DEDICATION 1

INTRODUCTION 5

CHAPTER 1 CALIFORNIA DREAMING 7

PART 1: Blowing In The Wind
(1967 – 1975)

CHAPTER 2 TELL IT LIKE IT IS 15

CHAPTER 3 I WISH WE'D ALL BEEN READY 25

CHAPTER 4 TAKE THE MESSAGE EVERYWHERE 37

CHAPTER 5 HIS EYE IS ON THE SPARROW 41

CHAPTER 6 HOME WHERE I BELONG 47

CHAPTER 7 GOD GAVE THE SONG 53

PART 2: The Times They Are A Changin'
(1976– 1984)

CHAPTER 8 WHAT A DIFFERENCE YOU'VE MADE 61

CHAPTER 9 THE SPIRIT MOVES 65

CHAPTER 10 HE'S ALIVE 69

CHAPTER 11 GOTTA TELL SOMEBODY 79

CHAPTER 12 I SURRENDER ALL 91

CHAPTER 13 ONE MORE SONG FOR YOU 101

CHAPTER 14 HEED THE CALL 109

CHAPTER 15 TAKING CARE OF BUSINESS 115
CHAPTER 16 THE GREAT DIVIDE 123
CHAPTER 17 MORE THAN WONDERFUL 131
CHAPTER 18 GOD GAVE ROCK 'N' ROLL TO YOU 137
CHAPTER 19 THIS MEANS WAR 145

PART 3: Gotta Serve Somebody (1985– 1995)

CHAPTER 20 TAKING IT TO THE STREETS 153
CHAPTER 21 COMIN' ON STRONG 159
CHAPTER 22 A NU THANG 167
CHAPTER 23 AND THE RACE IS ON 173
CHAPTER 24 WHEREVER HE LEADS I'LL GO 179
CHAPTER 25 MY TURN NOW 187
CHAPTER 26 OUR PLACE IN THIS WORLD 197
CHAPTER 27 A BRAND NEW START 205
CHAPTER 28 JUST SAY SO 215
CHAPTER 29 LOOKS LIKE WE MADE IT 221

EPILOGUE I CAN SEE CLEARLY NOW 229
THANK YOU'S 232

DEDICATION

The story of our lives—yours and mine—is being written every day. It is always a story of people living a dream, a tragedy or even the mundane passage of time—*together*. Life is designed to be lived *together* in harmony with people you love, admire and trust, even if it takes years to arrive at each of those conclusions.

I have spent much of my life in Contemporary Christian Music. But that experience would not have been possible without the efforts and sacrifice of many giants of our industry. They came before me, and many came alongside me, often when I didn't deserve their support or trust—men like Jarrell McCracken and Marvin Norcross who helped create Word Records in 1951. And men like Ralph Carmichael, Kurt Kaiser, and Billy Ray Hearn who had true vision for a "different sound" that would proclaim the love and person of Jesus Christ to my generation and beyond.

Incredibly, I began working with those great pioneers of Christian music as a 20-year-old college student. They each helped shape my life and a career that has now lasted over 40 years. Along the way I also met and began working alongside other great music pioneers, men like Bob Benson, Bob MacKenzie and Bill Gaither. All of these men are members of *my* Christian Music Hall of Fame.

My generation has produced some real heroes too. Top record industry executives of today like Jeff Moseley, Bill Hearn and Terry Hemmings continue to guide the development and distribution of the music. Agents, promoters, managers and visionaries like Chuck Tilley, Charles Dorris, John Huie, Dan Raines, Greg Ham, Chaz Corzine, Mike Atkins, Jeff Roberts, David Breen and many others still help deliver concerts and events that reach millions each year. And without executives like Darrell Harris, Michael Blanton, Peter York, Eddie DeGarmo, John Mays, Lynn Nichols, Neal Joseph and so many others who shaped the songs and performances that changed many lives, there would be no story to tell.

This book is filled with names you know—like Amy Grant, Michael W. Smith, Steven Curtis Chapman, Sandi Patty, Andrae Crouch, and Twila Paris—the singers, songwriters and performers whose creative contributions still encourage and inspire.

But without the behind-the-scenes work of the executives you'll meet here, that music might never have been heard. You need to know their names too: Roland Lundy, Dan Johnson, Allen Weed, Lynn Nichols, Danny McGuffey, Brenda Boswell, Tom Ramsey, Thurlow Spurr, Dan Brock, Jerry Park, Loren Balman, Jackie Patillo, Wayne Erickson, Gary Whitlock, Lynn Keesecker, Rick Horne, Bill Traylor, Norman Miller, Don Cason, Roger Breland, Phil Perkins, Rod Huff, John Styll, Jerry Weimer, Dan Harrell, Chuck Fromm and so many others.

To make the machine we call the Christian Music Industry run, it has also taken thousands of assistants, supervisors, designers, copywriters, accountants, administrators, IT folks and shipping clerks. Without friends like Don McCauley, Shirley Nowaski, Claudine Buchanan, Bull Mitchell, Alex

MacDougall, Jim Pippin, Bugsy Giglio, Sandy Cave, Dennis Hill, Piers Bateman, Tom Bates, Tracy Simmons and hundreds of others, we would not be having this discussion.

As you read these stories, I hope you'll also remember these dedicated men and women—just ordinary folks like me who needed a job, but often discovered a passion for this music. Without them, the songs and the artists who sing them so well would never have seen the light of day.

So this book is dedicated to all of you—the men and women who helped create the music, promote the songs, make the sales, run the reports, write the checks, answer the phones or pack and ship the albums, eight-tracks, cassettes and CDs.

Thank you for the music, the memories and the life-changing message of Contemporary Christian Music. And thank you for your friendship along the way.

THIS IS OUR STORY. THIS IS OUR PLACE...IN HISTORY.

INTRODUCTION

A BOOK LIKE THIS CANNOT BE WRITTEN UNTIL IT HAS BEEN LIVED.

Age is a wonderful thing—in some ways. It grants perspective that usually escapes a young person. The tyranny of the urgent has been a brutal taskmaster for much of my life. I always assumed there would be a time to reflect on my life. The only surprise is that the time has arrived far more quickly than I had expected.

What you are about to read really happened. This book is the "collective recollection" of a group of men and women who actually wrote the songs, recorded the music, broadcasted the music, promoted the concerts, and built the business structure we now call the Christian Music Industry. This story was not contrived, borrowed or embellished. It is the very real, behind-the-scenes eyewitness narrative of an era that produced a form of music that continues to impact millions of lives.

The reason I am telling this story is because I was there; I was there for the birth of a musical era that is still touching lives. And you need to know the many ways that God intervened in our lives to make that possible.

From the advent of the eight-track player in the Ford Mustang in 1965 to the first Sony Walkman cassette player in 1979 and the digital revolution that followed, the artists, songwriters and executives you are reading about in this book were all in the right place at the right time to impact millions of lives—and to build an industry in the process.

Only God knows why He gave me—and many others—key roles in developing Contemporary Christian Music, but He did. And by His grace we stood together and delivered the life-changing message of Christ to our generation and beyond.

I hope our story will encourage you to do the same.

Chapter 1

CALIFORNIA DREAMING

It's a long way from Waco, Texas, to Hollywood. Although I had made that trip many times during my career, March 21, 1985 was different. I was about to be part of history in a place with quite a history of its own.

Sitting at a red light on Sunset Boulevard, with the windows down and the slight ocean breeze drifting through my rental car, I could understand why so many people wanted to live in Southern California. Minutes later, I arrived at 1416 North La Brea Avenue, site of the movie studio that silent film star Charlie Chaplain had built in 1917.

Through the years, The *Adventures of Superman, Red Skelton, Perry Mason* and other hit TV shows had been filmed on the property. And then in the mid-60's Herb Alpert and Jerry Moss bought the place for their new music business venture, A&M Records. I'm even told that Harrison Ford, in his pre-movie star days, made a deal to do the woodwork for them.

A "deal" brought me to A&M Records that day as well. A deal that would change the Contemporary Christian Music industry—forever.

At the time, I was in charge of Word Records, the world's

largest Christian music company. Our artist roster was unprecedented. We sold a lot of records from artists like Al Green, The Mighty Clouds of Joy, The Happy Goodman Family, The Imperials, Bill Gaither, Petra and many other CCM stars of the day. But I was there that day because of one artist—Amy Grant.

Amy was the star attraction, the number one artist in Contemporary Christian Music. She performed for huge crowds night after night and even on national television at the recent Grammy Awards. Sales of her album ***Age to Age*** had surpassed every other Christian album of all time, and we had the RIAA certified Gold and Platinum Records to prove it. Her recent follow-up release ***Straight Ahead*** had already sold more than a million copies. And it was time for her next album to

▼ CELEBRATING AMY'S FIRST GOLD RECORD "AGE TO AGE"
Brown Bannister, Dan Johnson, Jarrell McCracken, Stan Moser, Amy Grant, Roland Lundy, Dan Harrell, Mike Blanton
© Word Music Entertainment

hit the streets.

It seemed that Amy's songs were always at the top of our Christian radio charts. And that success made it possible for us to sell millions of her albums through Christian retailers. And we had fought hard to get her music into the mainstream of American culture—with limited success. But after today, things would be different. Our new contract with A&M Records would soon help make Amy Grant a household name and shape the future of our entire industry.

A few months earlier, we had identified A&M as our ideal partner to take Contemporary Christian Music to the last real frontier for our music—pop radio. They were arguably the leading independent music company in the world. Not only did they make hit records for co-owner Herb Alpert, but also for Joan Baez, George Benson, Peter Frampton, The Police, Janet Jackson, Supertramp, Sting and many others. They also had the number one box office smash movie, ***The Breakfast Club***. And in Hollywood, nothing glows brighter than a hit movie.

A&M's president, Gil Friesen, and I had worked on the deal for months. The deal was really pretty simple. Amy's new album, ***Unguarded***, would be released simultaneously on our Myrrh label *and* on the A&M label. They would then deliver Amy to pop radio and general market retailers like Walmart, Tower Records, Musicland and KMart. We had no doubt. If A&M could get our music on the pop radio charts, Contemporary Christian Music would finally reach the masses.

Gil felt that the best way to launch our relationship was a lunch meeting in their famous Studio A, where he could play Amy's ***Unguarded*** album for his entire staff.

I walked from the parking lot into Studio A. The

wood-paneled, state-of-the-art studio was about 40 feet by 40 feet and had a 24-foot-high ceiling. That day it contained round tables of eight. As the A&M staff filed into the room, they struck me as tolerant, but really not all that interested. They had been through this song and dance before. But we didn't care. It was Amy's day; it was our day.

When everyone arrived, lunch was served. We all listened as Gil Friesen addressed his team. In his brief remarks, he said, "Today is one of the most significant days in the history of A&M Records." It was even more than that for Word Records, and for our entire industry; it was historic.

Amy sat to my right. Around the table were her managers, Mike Blanton and Dan Harrell, her producer Brown Bannister, and our Word/Myrrh team of Dan Johnson, Roland Lundy and Lynn Nichols. We had finally arrived in *every* sense of the word.

As I looked around, it hit me. We were making CCM history in the very room where "We Are The World," the most highly promoted single and music video in music industry history had been recorded just two months earlier.

Michael Jackson, Sting, Bob Dylan, Dionne Warwick, Huey Lewis, Diana Ross, Prince, Ray Charles, Billy Joel, Bruce Springsteen and so many other icons of pop music had stood right *here* as they recorded it.

Just getting a group of artists like that together in one room had been a massive logistical and artistic challenge. Producer Quincy Jones had wisely posted a sign at the entrance that told the stars, "Check your ego at the door." And from what I heard they did. The dream of helping change the lives of desperate and hungry people halfway around the world made it happen.

We had dreams too. After today, Contemporary Christian Music would soon be played on pop radio and placed front and center on the shelves of general market retailers. People around the world who desperately needed hope and encouragement would soon hear our life-changing message—Jesus *is* the way to the life they long for.

As I looked around the table I wondered, "How on earth did *we* get here?" How could a kid who grew up knowing nothing about the music business get from Waco, Texas, to the very place where music legends had made history just two months earlier?

While the music played, Amy leaned over to me and said, "You know what's really special about all this? Look around the table. The best part of all this is that we've all been together as friends from the very beginning, and we get to do this together too."

In that moment, Amy Grant delivered a message that I didn't really understand until almost 30 years later while I was writing this book. And you will soon understand too.

As I said, it's a long way from Waco to Hollywood, and it is a story well worth telling.

▲ FROM TOP LEFT: Andrae Crouch, Larry Norman, Evie, Pastor Chuck Smith, Love Song (Bob Wall, Tommy Coomes, John Mehler, Chuck Girard, Jay Truax), Barry McGuire, Phil Keaggy

BLOWING IN THE WIND

1967 –1975

Chapter 2
TELL IT LIKE IT IS

May 5, 1961, was just another day in my 11-year-old life. Or so I thought. As I grabbed my books and headed for the door my dad stopped me.

"You're not going to school right now." The reason he explained very simply, "We're all going to watch a man get launched into space. That's more important than work or school. Turn on the TV." I was as excited as an 11-year-old boy could be. Imagine, a human was going to be *blasted* into outer space.

In reality, America's first astronaut, Alan Shepard, would only ascend about a hundred miles high and then travel about 300 miles before splashing down just 17 minutes later. But those were meaningless details to me. All I knew is that I was about to see history in the making.

I watched our 19-inch black-and-white Sylvania television with my brother, Michael, and sister, Kay, as ABC-TV's Jules Bergman explained each step of the process. My eyes were glued to the screen as I watched Alan Shepard board the Transfer Vehicle, which transported him to the Mercury-Redstone Launch Vehicle—his space rocket. When he stepped into the elevator and closed the door, I swallowed hard. My mouth felt like cotton.

Seconds later, Shepard stepped off the elevator about 80 feet off the ground. He slowly examined the tiny Mercury capsule they called ***Freedom 7*** that would hopefully bring him back to Earth, and then stood still. *Was he afraid? How could he even fit in there?* Then I saw the men help him slide into those tight quarters. They closed and sealed the door.

My heart began pounding as I realized he was strapped to the top of an 80-foot-tall rocket that would carry him into space. According to the den clock, it was 8:33 a.m. when the off-screen voice started the countdown, "10...9...8...7..."

For 17 minutes we all held our breath, and then it was over for Commander Shepard. His place in history was settled forever. And in my 11-year-old mind the die for my future was cast—I was going to work for NASA and help launch astronauts into orbit. But as I would find out less than 10 years later, God had a different plan for my life.

DEEP IN THE HEART OF TEXAS

My hometown of Waco is a city of about 120,000 people right in the heart of Texas. It is or was home to Ann Richards, former Texas Governor, comedian and actor Steve Martin, worship leader Kari Jobe...and me.

Waco is cradled between the East Texas piney woods where I was born and the dry West Texas high plains. It can be one of those broiling furnace Texas towns in the summer, and Waco winters can be very cold. The city is also located in "Tornado Alley." In fact, in 1953, just two years before my family moved there, a tornado killed 114 people in the area.

Historically, most people have associated Waco with

Baylor University or even Dr Pepper, since that soft drink was birthed there. But Waco is also the original home of Word Records. And Word would soon become the launching pad for my career and a new form of music that would impact millions.

Our family was pretty normal from the outside. Church was a pivotal part of my life as a youngster. We were Southern Baptists. That meant we always showed up for Sunday school, Sunday night supper in the fellowship hall and prayer meeting on Wednesday night. Since I was an R.A. (Royal Ambassador), I didn't have to attend prayer meeting. I guess kids were exempt for some reason.

I remember the rituals of the Saturday night bath and polishing my shoes because we were going to Sunday school in the morning! And I am so grateful for the wonderful men and women who taught me the Bible. I still remember those flannel board stories. In fact, I got a gold star for perfect attendance when I was 12. Of course, that meant my parents had to find a church for me to attend as we traveled across the country on our family vacation. That gold star was important.

But when I became a teenager, the gold star and church in general lost their value for me. I had no youth group to hook me in with Xbox, PlayStation, Nintendo, catchy slogans, trips to Six Flags or pizza parties. There was no Contemporary Christian Music to make my time at church at least musically relevant. And the weekly curriculum just didn't relate to what I was going through.

As a teenager in the 60's, my world was filled with anything but love, peace and joy. The images of "free love," drug addiction, the inevitable nuclear war with Russia, and violence in the streets dominated the evening news. The musician poets on the radio kept looking for answers. But they were looking in all the wrong places.

I grew up much too fast. Like many kids who grew up in church, I lived two lives—the "good boy" that I allowed my parents and church folks to see, and the "sinner" that I really was. I believed that Jesus died for my sins and that when I had walked the aisle as a kid, I was saved. In other words, I had my ticket to heaven punched. But I didn't know much about the Bible, even after all those lessons in Sunday School.

The idea of just blowing church off as a teenager crossed my mind, but it never made sense. After all, I am human, and I have a deep need to belong somewhere. Besides, I didn't want to disappoint my parents.

My dad, Dr. L. E. Moser, was a professor at Baylor University, so naturally that's where I went to college. I majored in math and took a lot of courses in physics to prepare for my dream job at NASA. Now just to be clear, I definitely didn't want to be strapped on top of a rocket like Alan Shepard. I just wanted to be part of ground control and help launch a bunch of other guys into space.

I wasn't the only one fascinated with the idea of space travel. Shortly after his inauguration, President Kennedy made it clear: A United States astronaut would be the first to walk on the moon. That goal became a national obsession, and on July 20, 1969, it happened. Neil Armstrong walked on the moon.

Although there were five more Apollo missions over the next couple of years, funding for NASA and the space program began to dry up. I'm not sure exactly why that happened, but the career opportunity I had planned for nearly 10 years seemed to vanish.

What Commander Armstrong described as "one small step for man, one giant leap for mankind" turned out to be a backward step for my life plan. Working at NASA was no longer an option. I had less than two years to complete my degree and find a career.

IN THE BEGINNING WAS WORD

Back in 1967, when I was a senior in high school, Bill Glass, the Baylor football and NFL defensive end, co-authored a book with my dad. *Stand Tall and Straight* was written as a guide to manhood for teenage boys. It was not a best-seller, but it did introduce me to Word, the book publisher. In fact, I helped my dad and Bill Glass by adjusting the language to their target audience of teenage boys. They even shared author credit with me, a 17-year-old kid who was definitely not living the message of that book.

ANNOUNCING THE RELEASE OF "STAND TALL AND STRAIGHT."
Jarrell McCracken, Bill Glass, Stan Moser, Dr. L. E. Moser
© Word Music Entertainment

A great group of Southern gospel artists where on Word's Canaan Records label, including The Florida Boys, The Cathedral Quartet and The Happy Goodman Family

George Baskin was the editor for our book. So two years later, when I told my dad that I needed to find a part-time job that might have full-time potential in a few months, he suggested that I call George at Word. I did.

George, who had become Vice President of Marketing, hired me to do market research for Word's direct-to-consumer book and record clubs. I began working at Word, Inc. (the parent company of the Word Records label) on February 1, 1970, as a part-time, 20-year-old college student.

In those days, Word had a very successful record club that shipped a new album to members at least once a month. Club members had to return a "rejection notice" to the company or we would automatically ship them each new release. Vera Washburn's job was to separate the rejection slips by club (Family Record Club, Word Book Club, Canaan Record Club) and take them to the computer room to be scanned.

So my career started with sharing a rented folding table with Vera, the "reject girl," earning a whopping $1.60 per hour. We all have to start somewhere.

At that time, Word's big artists included Anita Bryant, Burl Ives, The Pat Boone Family, Norma Zimmer, Jim Roberts and Frank Boggs. Not exactly what a 20-year-old would listen to on his AM car radio.

We also had a great group of Southern gospel artists on our Canaan Records label. The Florida Boys, The Cathedral Quartet and The Happy Goodman Family sold a lot of records and paid much of our overhead. And we owned 50% of Light Records, which was founded by Ralph Carmichael. Ralph was a true pioneer in contemporary church music, but you had to actually go to church to know that. And for me, like most of my friends, church just wasn't on the radar.

The Beatles, The Rolling Stones, Janice Joplin, Bob Dylan, Simon & Garfunkel and others who definitely did not represent the values of the church shaped my generation. The music that had paid the bills at Word for the last two decades had no chance of impacting my generation, but that was about to change.

MORE ABOUT... RALPH CARMICHAEL

Before forming Light Records, Ralph Carmichael was a top arranger and producer in Hollywood music circles. His fame began as a student at what is now Vanguard University in Santa Ana, California. While still a student, Ralph won an Emmy for a weekly television show he produced at CBS Channel 2 in Los Angeles. His production credits range from Nat King Cole's biggest hits to music for many of Billy Graham's Worldwide Pictures releases.

For more than 60 years of great music, Ralph's simple vision has never wavered:

"I'm so grateful I found a way to communicate the gospel, but not just through preaching. I'm not a very good public speaker. I became a conductor so I could stand with my back to the audience!"

LET THERE BE LIGHT

Just one year earlier, Ralph Carmichael and Kurt Kaiser had produced a church youth musical called ***Tell It Like It Is***. It had shocked many church leaders. The church really needed to reach young people like me through the exploding medium of pop music. But before that could happen, church leaders would have to see that God could use guitars and drums.

LIGHT
RECORDS

The release of *Tell It Like It Is* on Ralph Carmichael's Light Records label in early 1969 was just the beginning of a musical earthquake inside the church.

The release of ***Tell It Like It Is*** on Ralph Carmichael's Light Records label in early 1969 was just the beginning of a musical earthquake inside the church. Other landmark youth musicals like Kurt and Ralph's ***Natural High*** and Jimmy and Carol Owens' ***Come Together*** soon followed. Before long, Light Records became home to Andrae Crouch and the Disciples and ultimately many other successful contemporary and gospel music artists.

Kurt and Ralph's songs and arrangements revolutionized church music. But the unseen driving force behind the contemporary church music movement was a man named Billy Ray Hearn. By the mid 1960's, Billy Ray had a rapidly growing influence in the church music world. From playing the violin as a young boy to serving as music and choir director at several Southern Baptist churches across Texas and Georgia, Billy Ray moved into a lifelong career of reaching young people for Christ.

GOOD NEWS

In 1967, while serving as Minister of Music at First Baptist Church in Thomasville, Georgia, Billy Ray helped put his vision for contemporary church music on paper. That vision became a contemporary church musical called ***Good News***. Somehow, the Baptist Sunday School Board chose to publish what would become a controversial songbook, complete with those evil guitar chords!

Billy Ray was driven to succeed because he had personally witnessed the impact of the gospel on young people in his church when delivered in a musical style they could embrace. Being a great promoter, he fearlessly took on a church establishment that was determined to keep drums and guitars ("instruments of the devil") out of the church. That drive never waned no matter how many barriers he faced.

▼ Billy Ray Hearn
© Word Music Entertainment

When he was invited to bring his choir to the 1968 annual Southern Baptist Convention meeting in Houston, Texas, Billy Ray decided it was time to make a statement. He added 50 guitar players to a stage filled with 17 youth choirs from 11 different states, and they performed ***Good News*** right before Billy Graham delivered the evening message to more than 10,000 staunch Southern Baptists.

Soon Jarrell McCracken, President of Word Records, invited Billy Ray to move to Waco and help create and promote a growing line of contemporary church music. That move positioned Billy Ray to bring his vision to a nationwide audience. It didn't take long for Billy Ray to connect with Ralph Carmichael and Kurt Kaiser. ***Tell It Like It Is*** would soon follow.

Billy Ray's vision for music that would impact young people was contagious. Ralph had been arranging and recording highly successful traditional church music for decades, but when he realized his own teenage daughter would sneak into the garage during the night and listen to rock music on the car radio, he knew it was time to create a whole new sound.

When ***Tell It Like It Is*** hit the market in 1969, church music began a long journey to relevance for my generation, even though I didn't have a clue. As I said, I was a teenager who had left the church behind. No youth group. No youth choir. No pastor. Just a mother and father who raised me right and implanted a belief that I could succeed in life.

My deepest "spiritual" experience in those days occurred while listening to an eight-track tape of Simon & Garfunkel singing "Bridge Over Troubled Water" while cruising in my 1967 Pontiac GTO. As it turned out, I would need a long bridge over some very troubled waters in my life over the next three decades—right in the midst of being a part of music and church history.

Chapter 3
I WISH WE'D ALL BEEN READY

While Ralph, Kurt and Billy Ray were shocking leaders in the church world with *Tell It Like It Is*, another type of Christian music—Jesus Music—was being birthed on the beaches, parks and sidewalks of Southern California. The Jesus Movement had begun.

As the hippy generation of the late 60's failed to find the "serenity and peace" that their counterculture lifestyle had promised, many surrendered their lives to Christ. Upon doing so, their lifestyle began to change, but their music style did not. Artists like Love Song, Larry Norman, and Randy Stonehill began to write and perform songs about their newfound faith in Jesus. Many others followed.

Many of the early Jesus Music pioneers were inspired by Larry Norman's song from 1969, "I Wish We'd All Been Ready." Larry was a fairly new Christian whose music career already included opening for The Doors and Jimi Hendrix. Larry knew the power of music to sway his generation toward good or evil. His musical lament about the return of Christ created urgency in many newly born-again Jesus Movement musicians to let their music reflect their faith.

THE SOUND OF CHANGE

At the age of 40, Chuck Smith had given up ministry. Nothing he did seemed to work, so he went to work at a supermarket in Southern California.

But everything in his life changed when some of the teenagers he had tried to pastor asked him to come to the beach one day. They had been witnessing to the hippies on that beach and many were giving their lives to Christ. The kids didn't know what to do next, but they knew Pastor Chuck would.

Over the next few weeks, Chuck baptized hundreds of hippies and began teaching them basic Biblical truths. And the former Foursquare pastor who had given up on ministry soon gave new leadership to Calvary Chapel in Costa Mesa, California. It became "the" gathering place for those hippies.

As a true visionary, he saw the value of the music coming from talented musicians who had been radically changed by Christ. In 1970, the church featured that music during an outreach at Huntington Beach High School. The response was overwhelming; kids came to Christ and many even turned in their drugs. Everyone could see that the music was crucial to what happened there.

That's when Pastor Smith knew they had to "bottle" that sound for others. The explosive growth of recording technology made it possible in ways that had not existed a few years earlier.

So while we were learning how to sell Jesus Music in Waco, Calvary Chapel's Maranatha!Music was *making* Jesus Music history in Southern California.

The first Maranatha album released in 1971 was a compilation of songs entitled ***The Everlastin' Living Jesus Music Concert***. Over the next few years, the label launched recordings from many of the artists who came to define Jesus Music. Songs from Daniel Amos, Sweet Comfort Band, Children of the Day, Ernie and Debbie Rettino, Oden Fong, Mustard Seed Faith and Parable helped shape an entire generation of new Christians.

For Pastor Chuck, the label was never about making money. It was always about the gospel and the opportunity for newly born-again musicians to express their faith and spread the love of Jesus Christ. Calvary Chapel's Saturday night concert and evangelistic services led by Tom Stipe soon combined the music of a new generation with an open invitation to new life in Christ. Thousands responded.

From its humble beginnings, surrounded by hippie vans and hosting thousands of young people who didn't have a clue about the Christian life, Calvary Chapel became a thriving ministry that lives on today through more than 1,000 churches located around the world.

FROM A CALIFORNIA BEACH TO WACO, TEXAS

At Word, we were certainly aware of the Jesus Music coming out of California (most notably through Calvary Chapel), but it was an enigma to our Southern Baptist culture. I wasn't in charge at that point, but I'm confident that Jarrell, Marvin and even Kurt were not sure where or if we should dive in.

Fortunately, Billy Ray Hearn was absolutely certain that Word needed to be in the Jesus Music business. In 1970, he received a demo tape from Monty Matthews, one of the original members of The Jordanaires. That tape featured Monty's son, Randy, playing what many church leaders of that day would call "drug-oriented hippie music." In 1971, Randy Matthews' album, appropriately titled ***Wish We'd All Been Ready***, became the first nontraditional album released on Word Records. The battle for acceptance in the church was fierce.

As Billy Ray remembers, "Randy *was* radical; some people thought he was evil. He went to a lot of music festivals and sang anywhere he could. At one festival in the Midwest, someone in charge pulled the plugs on his amplifiers!" The resistance to Randy Matthews pushed Billy Ray to find other ways to get contemporary music past church leaders.

Billy Ray understood that music comes out of the culture. Looking back on that period, he said, "Throughout history, every style of music has come that way into the church. At first it's totally rejected, then it's tolerated and then it's accepted. The hippies, the street kids, didn't find all they expected in their peace movements. But a bunch of them found Jesus and wrote songs about Him. That was a reflection of their culture—their 'new' culture. So we were putting the gospel into commercial music, and it reached people who needed it."

As you can imagine, the "radical" contemporary music Billy Ray was determined to produce didn't sit very well with our traditional Word audience; it's a long way from Frank Boggs and Norma Zimmer to Randy Matthews. There was just no way to put them on the same label. So Billy Ray went to Jarrell McCracken and made it clear that this "new music" needed its own home since it just didn't fit with the more traditional Word label. Jarrell didn't agree but Billy Ray was relentless. In 1972 Myrrh Records, a division of Word Records, was born.

myrrh Records

In 1972 Myrrh Records, a division of Word Records, was born.

Contemporary church music

(as we called it then) was alive, but not so well in those early days. Billy Ray brought us singles and albums from Randy Matthews, Dust, Crimson Bridge, Ray Repp, Ray Hildebrand, Honeytree, First Gear, and Ron Salsbury and the J.C. Power Outlet. I had started Word's telephone sales department by that time (the term "telemarketing" had not yet been coined), but there just weren't many buyers for those early albums.

While attending a Nancy Honeytree concert in Fort Wayne, Indiana, Billy Ray was introduced to a radical Christian rock band called Petra. He brought two Petra albums to Myrrh, but we couldn't figure out how to sell them either. Ultimately, they moved on to the upstart Star Song label and became the number one Christian rock band of all time. Our paths would cross again a few years later.

A NEW CHAPTER

While building the Myrrh label, Billy Ray also continued his role as promotion manager for our choral print music products. The key to making a youth musical succeed was holding "choral music workshops" that attracted hundreds of choir directors to come and hear the company's music.

About that same time, Light Records introduced a new youth musical (for the same market as ***Tell It Like It Is***) called ***Come Together***. Billy Ray invited Jimmy and Carol Owens, the creators and writers of ***Come Together***, to bring their team from California to perform at a large music workshop we were hosting at Baylor's Waco Hall.

Their team included Pat Boone as the narrator and featured soloists Annie Herring and her little brother, Matthew Ward. Billy Ray recalls, "When I heard Annie and Matthew sing, I couldn't believe it. It gave me chills. When I heard the story of how Annie and Buck (her husband) took her younger brother Matthew and sister Nellie in after their parents tragically died, I knew this was something we needed to get involved with."

But Annie's husband, Buck Herring, had different plans. As a former Top 40 DJ, he was convinced that they needed to be on a secular label. As Buck said, "We want to sing to the public, not the choir." However, Buck introduced Billy Ray to another brand-new Christian recording artist who had "sung to the public" quite well. His name was Barry McGuire. And our sales team had its first significant selling artist on the Myrrh label.

DID YOU KNOW?

Billy Ray's wife, Joan, actually named the Myrrh label. She felt that the music released through Myrrh was meant to be "OUR GIFT TO JESUS."

Buck took their group, Second Chapter of Acts (sisters Nellie and Annie and their brother Matthew), to a secular label started by Pat Boone in conjunction with MGM Records and his friend Mike Curb. Second Chapter hit it big when their second single, called "I'm So Happy," soared up the charts to become a top-five single, but Buck found that he didn't like working with a secular record label.

Buck sent an unreleased version of a new album to Billy Ray to see if he might still be interested in signing Second Chapter. That album included "Easter Song," and it didn't take Billy Ray long to agree to release their new album, ***With***

Footnotes, on Myrrh in 1974. The impact of "Easter Song" on radio and across the church forced Christian retailers to put ***With Footnotes*** front and center in their record sections. That was a huge windfall for us in the sales department.

Undeniably, Billy Ray had something very special with Second Chapter and Barry McGuire. Retailers began to pay attention when our sales reps presented new Myrrh releases. We were also experiencing great gains at a small number of Christian radio stations — those who had the nerve to play contemporary music.

The Word Records that loyal customers had known for more than two decades was changing before their eyes. Soon an event in Dallas, Texas, in the summer of 1972 brought thousands of young people face to face with the music that would ultimately impact millions of listeners around the world.

▼ EXPLO '72 INTRODUCED JESUS MUSIC TO THOUSANDS OF NEW FANS.

Explo '72, sponsored by Campus Crusade, drew more than 100,000 people, and artists like Love Song, Larry Norman, Randy Matthews, and Andrae Crouch would soon become household names. The Jesus Music explosion had begun. Without Billy Ray's vision and determination, we might have missed this great opportunity.

NOTHING HAPPENS UNTIL SOMEBODY SELLS SOMETHING

In November of 1974, my boss, Francis "Doc" Heatherley, our VP of Sales and Marketing, left Word to become President of Vision House Publishers in California. Jarrell reluctantly promoted me as his replacement, saying I was the only choice he had. I could have used a bit more encouragement, but the $2,500 per year raise he gave me certainly helped pay the bills.

At 24 years old, I was suddenly managing men twice my age, many of whom were paid more than three times what I

MORE ABOUT...ROLAND LUNDY

ROLAND BEGAN HIS CAREER AT WORD as a telephone salesman in 1972. When I became Sales Manager, promoting Roland to Assistant Sales Manager seemed like a no-brainer to me. His Word career lasted 29 years, culminating in his role as President of the company (including music and book divisions) in 1989. And he became one of the greatest executives our industry has ever known. I wish every decision I made had worked out so well!

was making. I was in charge of the largest sales organization in the Christian music business, and I needed wisdom badly. But by that point, I had not been part of the local church for nearly 10 years, and the Bible was the last place I would have turned for wisdom or counsel.

But I did make at least one good decision. I hired Roland Lundy.

Roland and I didn't realize it at the time, but we had just begun a lifelong friendship and career that would be driven by the convergence of four historically unique elements:

1. **The Jesus Movement:** God's response to the counterculture nature of the hippie generation.

2. **The Charismatic Renewal:** A powerful move of God that birthed or revived countless ministries and churches including Calvary Chapel, Vineyard, Church on the Way and so many more.

3. **The Church Youth Group Explosion:** The rapid expansion

A SIGN OF THINGS TO COME

Over the next few years, Word would change dramatically. One change, however, altered the landscape of the Christian music industry. On November 21, 1974, American Broadcasting Company, Inc., the parent company of ABC Television, bought Word.

The future of Christian music changed that day. The capital and the distribution systems that a major corporation like ABC brought to the table would help us expand the Christian music market, but transferring ownership of songs like "The Old Rugged Cross" and "In The Garden" into secular hands created a lot of controversy in the church.

Over the next 20 years, every other major Christian music company would follow suit. It seemed to be the only way to reach the masses with this life-changing music.

of Youth Groups and Youth Choirs in mainstream, charismatic and evangelical churches.

4. The Technology Revolution: Evolving electronic and digital advances that enabled the creation, exposure, mobilization and personal utilization of music.

With the release of Second Chapter's ***With Footnotes***, our sales team was fully in the Jesus Music business. We soon began selling albums from artists like Love Song, Chuck Girard, Larry Norman and Randy Stonehill that we picked up through distribution deals with smaller labels like Solid Rock Records and Good News Records.

Christian retailers were beginning to see that promoting Jesus Music could bring new customers into their stores. But a preacher's kid in California named Andrae Crouch and a teenage girl named Evie Tornquist from New Jersey delivered the biggest impact on our sales. Their careers coincided with the rise of the Jesus Movement, and their success would soon force us to find a new name for their music.

FROM ONE PIONEER TO ANOTHER

Shortly after the success of ***Tell It Like It Is***, Ralph Carmichael got a game-changing phone call from Tim Spencer, a founding member of the historic Western music group Sons of the Pioneers. Ralph's passion for creating ***Tell It Like It Is*** had been driven by his desire to communicate the gospel through music to young people, including his own daughter. Tim Spencer was about to introduce him to a young man who would become one of the best musical communicators of all time.

That young man was Andrae Crouch. Ralph just loved Andrae's touch on the piano, his chord progressions, and of course, his great lyrics. It didn't take long for Andrae to become a Light Records artist and the number one selling contemporary artist for our entire Word sales team.

Just a couple of years later, another phone call opened a huge door for Kurt Kaiser and our Word sales team. One of Word's very traditional artists, The Palermo Brothers, told Kurt about an amazing 17-year-old girl named Evie who sang with them from time to time.

Kurt went to hear Evie in concert and promptly decided to record her for the Word label. Over the next few years, we sold more than 2,000,000 Evie Tornquist albums. I think Kurt made a good decision.

CELEBRATING EVIE'S AUSTRALIAN GOLD RECORDS WITH THE WORD TEAM

Like most music pioneers, Andrae and Evie did not come from a predictable mold. Andrae lived in California and grew up in the church, a pastor's son. He definitely was not a hippie who found Jesus on the beach one night. Many people thought Evie came from Sweden, but she grew up in a staunch Assembly of God church family in Rahway, New Jersey. The Jesus Music label just didn't fit either one.

It was time for a new plan—a new name, and two very significant record labels to be created. Jesus Music was about to move over. Contemporary Christian Music would soon sweep the nation and the world.

▼ RALPH CARMICHAEL & STAN MOSER CELEBRATE THE SUCCESS OF THE "HE'S EVERYTHING TO ME PLUS 53" SONGBOOK SERIES.
"My mother, Ruth Moser, was the finest musician I have ever known. Ralph Carmichael was her favorite musician. This autographed picture was one of her treasures while she was here on earth. Every time I see it, I'm reminded of her love for Jesus." © Word Music Entertainment

Chapter 4

TAKE THE MESSAGE EVERYWHERE

Our success with Andrae and Evie changed the direction of our company and ultimately the entire industry. They were the cornerstones of what would soon become known as Contemporary Christian Music.

Andrae's success set the stage for many artists and songwriters. He was the gold standard for classic contemporary Christian songs. I still remember the day I first heard Andrae's albums ***Take The Message Everywhere*** and ***Keep On Singing***. To my 20-something ears, it was just a Christian version of the "soul music" that Motown Records delivered to pop radio. Finally, I had heard Christian music my friends just might listen to. As I listened, the life-changing messages embedded in those songs slowly began to impact even me.

Evie was simply, Evie. I'm still amazed that a solo artist, singing mostly to pre-recorded tracks, could hold the attention of an audience of thousands. But Evie could and did. There was just something special about her smile, her stories and of course her songs.

The sale of Evie and Andrae's records allowed us to expand our distribution organization, paving the way for future albums. By 1976, Roland Lundy became our national sales manager with 24 field sales reps across the country. Our unspoken strategy was to find music that people wanted and put it where Christians shopped including pop record stores and big retailers like Kmart. That strategy never changed.

As our success with Andrae and Evie mushroomed, our main competition, the Benson Company in Nashville, began to sell a more contemporary sound from the longtime Southern gospel group, The Imperials, along with new releases from Reba Rambo and Dallas Holm. The trend was clear: first Andrae, then Evie and now The Imperials. It was time to create a whole new brand name to describe this fresh and growing genre of music.

DID YOU KNOW?

Many of Evie's songs were written by Ron Harris and Stormie O'Martian, the best-selling author of The Power of a Praying Wife and many other books.

MAKE IT MEAN SOMETHING

At that time the Family Record Club was one of Word's most successful ventures. Jarrell McCracken had started this direct-to-consumer sales program in the late 1950's, and we had a large direct-mail customer list. As Evie and Andrae's sales began to skyrocket, Bill Gohring, who ran our direct mail division, decided it was time to add a "contemporary division" to the club that featured mostly traditional artists and hymns.

At the time, our direct sales brochures were created by The Russ Reid Agency in Los Angeles. That meant Dan Johnson, our account rep with the agency, was about to arrive in

Waco to show us the strategy for launching the new contemporary music club.

On a seemingly typical summer day in 1975, Word's Advertising Manager, Piers Bateman, called a meeting for the purpose of naming that new contemporary music club. Since I was head of marketing and sales for Word's music division, he asked me to help lead the meeting.

There were only seven of us at the table that day: Piers, Roland Lundy, Dan Johnson, our Myrrh promotion man Frank Edmondson (aka Paul Baker on the radio), along with Andrea Miller (aka Noni Thompson in her single days) and Jim Breeden, both of whom were part of our church music division. We were just doing our job that morning; we did not know we were making history.-

The brochure designs that Dan brought to the meeting were really good. The only problem was we had no name for this new club because we had no name for this new music.

I began my part of the meeting by writing three words across the top page of my yellow pad: Contemporary Christian Music. Then I said, "What we have here is Contemporary Christian Music, but that terminology will never work. It's just too long and not very cool." Or something like that.

From there we brainstormed better ways to describe this new type of music. I wrote every idea we had on that yellow pad. By the end of the meeting, we had a different idea on every line. Finally, I put my pen down and stated the obvious, "It's pretty clear that none of these names work. I guess we'll just have to call it Contemporary Christian Music and make that mean something." For the next 10 years, we did just that, and along the way, our direct marketing team launched one of Word's most successful ventures: a new record club called The Music Connection.

Chapter 5

HIS EYE IS ON THE SPARROW

We saw an avalanche of new Contemporary Christian Music artists and songs over the next few years. As Evie, Andrae and The Imperials continued to sell records, Star Song began to sell Phil Keaggy, Rez Band and even Petra records after we released the band from Myrrh. The Benson Company in Nashville responded with a best-selling Reba Rambo album, *Lady* on its new contemporary Greentree label and soon followed that with Dallas Holm's Live album featuring one of the greatest songs in CCM history, "Rise Again."

Looking back on this era, it seems like God was moving so powerfully through Contemporary Christian Music that we just had to show up to succeed. In the sales department we adopted the motto "stack 'em high and watch 'em buy!" That strategy produced a lot of income for Word and a lot of new Contemporary Christian Music fans.

My whole focus was on building my own career, and I'm sure I let everybody around me know just how important I was. We really *were* delivering Christian music to those searching for hope and peace and confidence about the future. But beneath my outwardly confident exterior I was searching for that same hope and peace in my life.

As long as the sales numbers met our goals each month, I was large and in charge, but inwardly I still hadn't surrendered my life to Christ, in spite of my walk down the aisle as a six-year-old boy 20 years earlier.

By the end of 1976, we had doubled our sales of records and print music. Business was great, but God was setting me up for an encounter just a few months down the road that would change my life forever. And I didn't have a clue what was coming.

GO WEST YOUNG MAN

In 1975, my first boss at Word, George Baskin, moved to California to help start a new Christian book company called Acton House. After getting settled in his new role, George invited Billy Ray Hearn to move to Los Angeles and start a new label. George said they would finance it. Finally, Billy Ray could build his own team to fulfill the call God had placed on his life. He would soon create a home where he could produce, in his own words, "quality Christian music by artists who were living the life they were singing about."

Billy Ray believed that he had fallen off track with much of the recording we were doing at Word/Myrrh. He said later, "We got into doing records for the wrong reason. We were recording people just to sell records. When I met people like Second Chapter of Acts, Barry McGuire and The Talbot Brothers, my vision for reaching people for Christ was renewed. I truly believed that if you make records for the right reason, the result would be good sales."

That unshakable belief was the foundation for Sparrow Records that Billy Ray formed in early 1976. Two of his first artists were John and Terry Talbot. Billy Ray had met them the year before while at Myrrh, so he gave them the option of signing with his new and unproven label, or the more established Myrrh label. They chose Sparrow instantly, saying, "We don't want to sign with a company where we don't know anybody." As one who picked up a lot of the pieces of Myrrh after Billy Ray left, I believe they made the right choice. They had no champion at Myrrh; I believe they would have been miserable there.

SPARROW®

Billy Ray Hearn said
"I truly believed that if you make records for the right reason, the result would be good sales."

That unshakable belief was the foundation for Sparrow Records that Billy Ray formed in early 1976.

Billy Ray set up Sparrow in a low cost warehouse area in Canoga Park, California. He had learned a lot at Word about spending vs. income, and he also realized that the artists (mostly Jesus Music at that time) would not be comfortable coming to a high-rise executive office anyway.

Before long, Sparrow released "Reborn" by the Talbot Brothers as well as their solo projects. Second Chapter of Acts still owed Myrrh two records, so Billy Ray did the next best thing: He released solo recordings by lead singers Annie Herring and Matthew Ward. He also added former Myrrh artist Barry McGuire to the Sparrow roster. Barry quickly became Sparrow's best-selling artist.

Billy Ray had always understood contemporary church music, and during the early years of Sparrow, he created the Birdwing imprint to house amazing choral and worship projects like John Michael Talbot's "The Lord's Supper" and "The

Painter." Distributing additional projects such as Agape Force's "Music Machine" paid a lot of bills as well.

By 1977 Sparrow Records was beginning to thrive. But when the board at Acton House decided to sell the company to ABC, Billy Ray faced the unpleasant possibility that he might be working for Word once again. At that point, in a strange twist, he was given the option of buying Sparrow before that could happen. All he needed was $150,000 plus the ability to pay out another $300,000 over the next six years.

That was a lot of money in 1977. But with the help of his friend Tony Solerno, who ran Agape Force, Billy Ray soon became the sole owner of Sparrow Records.

FOR HIM WHO HAS EARS

1977 was also a good year for new artists under Sparrow. Scott Wesley Brown and Danniebelle Hall (former backup singer for Andrae Crouch) came on board that year, and both were successful. But the most significant signing that year was a young musician originally from Brooklyn, New York.

Terry Talbot, who was recording his first solo record for Sparrow, suggested that Billy Ray meet his piano player, Keith Green. So Billy Ray dropped by the studio and was simply overwhelmed by Keith's talent. When Keith invited him to a concert that Friday night at a small church in Sherman Oaks, Billy Ray immediately agreed to meet him there.

At the concert, Billy Ray came face to face with one of the most powerful and unusual artists Christian music had ever seen. He told me, "There were so many people that I couldn't get in the door. So I literally crawled through people's legs, down the aisle. He played an old piano and sang. It was incredible; sounded like a whole orchestra. After he finished, I crawled out and found Keith."

Billy Ray knew what he had just witnessed. "I have to sign you to my new label. Let's meet tomorrow at Shoney's." At breakfast, Billy Ray wrote out the contract terms on a napkin. The deal was done, but the music was just beginning.

Keith Green was one of those rare prophetic artists who lived his message. He hit the music business with his piano-banging style, confrontational lyrics and a profound passion for meeting the needs of the hurting people around him.

Rather than charge admission, Keith just passed KFC buckets during many concerts. Some attendees placed valuables in the buckets. As our former Word sales rep, Gill Few, recalls, "One time someone put a really nice camera with a telephoto lens in the bucket. When Keith found out, he somehow tracked down the kid who donated it and returned it with an admonition to always take photos that would bring glory to God."

Keith's first Spar-

DID YOU KNOW?

As new believers in 1975, Keith and Melodie Green began a personal outreach of inviting the broken and needy into their home (soon to be known as "The Greenhouse") in Los Angeles, using their income from CBS Records as support. When they ran out of space, they purchased the home next door and rented five more in the same neighborhood. This ministry to drug addicts, prostitutes and the homeless became known as Last Days Ministries.

row album ***For Him Who Has Ears to Hear*** was released in 1977 and was followed in 1978 by ***No Compromise***. Even today, his fans remember the "challenge, the indictment and the call" in those albums. Others remember the "bold, unashamed, honest, heartfelt and heart-rending" lyrics.

While Sparrow was taking root in Canoga Park, I was in the midst of our own explosive growth in Central Texas at Word. The CCM revolution was gaining momentum in retail stores, countless new radio stations, and concerts and festivals all across the country. However, after Billy Ray Hearn left, our product development department was simply not prepared to handle the incredible surge of Contemporary Christian Music.

For Roland, Dan and me there was only one answer to that problem: We signed distribution deals with smaller labels that were making the music that consumers wanted. But help was on the way.

One of those smaller labels we distributed was Pat Boone's Lamb and Lion Records. As I listened to Lamb and Lion's latest recording by a group named Dogwood, I knew that whoever produced that music was the real deal. I just had to meet that producer. Before long I was face to face with a young man who would become Word's first great producer of Contemporary Christian Music. His name was Chris Christian.

Chapter 6

HOME WHERE I BELONG

Imagine one of the biggest pop stars of your generation for a moment… maybe Sinatra, Michael Jackson, Celine Dion, Prince or Justin Bieber. Now imagine what would happen if that star became a Christian – right in the midst of a string of #1 hits – and joined the CCM world.

That's what it looked like to me when I walked into our conference room one morning in 1976 and saw B.J. Thomas standing there. Along with his wife, Gloria, and his pastor, he told us his dramatic conversion experience.

At the conclusion of his astonishing testimony, it was obvious to all of us. B.J. Thomas was going to make a record for Myrrh.

B.J. had been an established and very successful pop star for over a decade. He had 20 #1 hits including "Raindrops Keep Falling On My Head," "Another Somebody Done Somebody Wrong Song," "Eyes Of A New York Woman," "Hooked On A Feeling," and "I Just Can't Help Believing." Not bad for a boy who started out playing the bar circuit in South Texas.

At the time, B.J. was under contract to ABC Records, so we needed permission to record him. Jarrell McCracken called the President of ABC Records, Jerry Rubenstein. Jarrell shared the dramatic story of B.J.'s surrender to Christ and our desire to produce a Christian album with him. Jerry was unmoved. He quickly responded with, "You can do whatever you want with that guy! The last time he was in my office he was so high he turned over my desk when he left the room…literally!"

> **DID YOU KNOW?**
>
> **In 1975, while on the way to a concert in Hawaii, B.J. Thomas took nearly 80 pills and almost died. When he woke up in the hospital, he asked a nurse why he was still alive. She responded, "God must want you to accomplish more here in this world." That was the catalyst for his conversion the following year.**

A NEW DIRECTION

After leaving that meeting with B.J., I knew we had a unique opportunity. I also knew we could not turn to our usual list of record producers for this project. I immediately called Chris Christian.

When I met Chris a few months earlier at Mike Curb's house in Los Angeles, I learned that he had an extensive background in pop music as a writer and performer. There was no doubt in my mind that Chris had the pop music skills to produce B.J.'s album.

The next week we wired $40,000 to Chris. Our first B.J. Thomas record was underway and Contemporary Christian Music was about to take another giant step forward.

As Chris began working on B.J.'s record, I found myself

MORE ABOUT...CHRIS CHRISTIAN

As a sophomore at Abilene Christian College, Chris Smith decided to go to Nashville to see if he could find a place in the music industry. He soon found himself playing banjo for a Wayne Newton television special at the Opryland theme park. Soon after that, Newton invited Chris to Las Vegas to play in his show there.

When Elvis Presley recorded one of Chris' early songs, he discovered that ASCAP already had a Chris Smith on its roster. Since his middle name was Christian, he quickly became known as Chris Christian.

His artist career began when Mike Curb asked Chris to join Darryl Cotton and Michael Lloyd to form the group Cotton, Lloyd and Christian. Ultimately Chris wrote and recorded three top 10 pop singles as a solo artist, but Chris' real passion was writing and producing music that could reach the world with the gospel. That passion led to a career that included producing albums from The Imperials, B.J. Thomas, Dan Peek, and the Gaither Vocal Band, as well as signing and producing albums by Whiteheart, Amy Grant, Steve Archer, Mark Heard and Luke Garrett.

at the office late one night with a rare opportunity to clean off my desk. As I did, I found a test pressing of a new artist we had signed. I normally didn't listen to test pressings since we had plenty of staff to handle that. But for some reason I put our

Two amazing CCM artists and the Word executive team.
Evie and B.J. Thomas with Stan Moser, Roland Lundy, Dan Johnson
© Word Music Entertainment

new album from the Pat Terry Group on the turntable. Soon, I noticed a song that was buried on side two. I played "Home Where I Belong" over and over; it moved me to tears. The next day I called Chris and told him I had found *the* song for the new B.J. Thomas record. Since there were not many CCM songwriters or publishers, Chris wrote the majority of the rest of the album including the song, "Without a Doubt."

Just a few months later, B.J.'s first CCM album, ***Home Where I Belong***, flew to the top of the Christian music charts. I saw B.J.'s concert seven times in various settings during the first year following the release of that album. It was inspiring to watch him sing to gamblers and drunks in a Vegas lounge and then tell them about his new life with Jesus Christ. They all listened with great respect as he sang "Home Where I Belong" and other Christian songs before his signature "Raindrops." I talked to some of those people in those Vegas shows, and I know they heard the truth of the gospel.

After witnessing such a life-giving experience, it was sad to hear the stories of Christians booing B.J. at concerts simply because he performed his Christian songs in the midst of his pop music. B.J. was wounded deeply.

Through B.J.'s painful experience, I learned that we produced and sold four distinct kinds of Christian music:

- PREACHERS WHO SING
  (e.g. Kenneth Copeland, Jimmy Swaggart)
- SINGERS WHO PREACH
  (e.g. Mylon LeFevre, Steve Camp, Keith Green)
- CHRISTIANS WHO SING
  (most CCM artists you would recognize)
- SINGERS WHO ARE CHRISTIAN
  (e.g. B.J., Ricky Skaggs, Glen Campbell)

Once we learned that difference, we did a better job of promoting and marketing pop artists like B.J. to CCM fans. I wish I had known then what I know now. We could have done a better job of helping them understand.

Chapter 7

GOD GAVE THE SONG

As with any music, many talented people behind the curtain shaped the songs and recordings that made CCM famous. Throughout the history of Contemporary Christian Music, A&R (Artists & Repertoire) executives such as Billy Ray Hearn, Darrell Harris, Neal Joseph, Michael Blanton, John Mays, Lynn Nichols and Peter York listened to songs in rough form and worked with the songwriters, arrangers and producers like Chris Christian to perfect their craft.

Bill Gaither told me years ago, "A good song is written. A great song is re-written!" Somebody has to oversee that process. It all starts with the song. A skilled A&R executive knows how to match those songs with the right artist and producer.

Beginning with that first B.J. Thomas recording, Chris Christian became one of the most pivotal producers in the early days of CCM. Chris was a refreshing combination of artist, producer, songwriter and businessman who became a good personal friend. Chris achieved great impact in our industry with his musical talents and as an executive through his own label, Home Sweet Home Records. And along the way, he introduced us all to a young songwriter and future legendary CCM producer named Brown Bannister.

Due to the success of Andrae, Evie and our Canaan Record label, we built the most effective sales and distribution system in the industry. When Roland Lundy and I took over the sales team in 1974, we had 11 music sales reps. Just two years later we had grown to 24 salesmen across the country. We knew how to deliver the music to the rapidly expanding CCM fan base, and it didn't take long for the biggest CCM group at Benson to notice.

NO SHORTAGE OF TALENT—IN NASHVILLE

The Imperials were formed in 1964 and became a very successful Southern gospel quartet on Benson's Heartwarming label. As the members of The Imperials changed over the years, their music also evolved, and Benson was smart enough to move the group to their Impact label. When Sherman Andrus and Terry Blackwood joined Jim Murray and Armond Morales in 1974, the group's sound underwent a radical transformation; they were on their way to becoming the first major CCM group.

Their 1975 release, ***No Shortage***, sold 50,000 units through the Benson Company. In those days, that was a huge-selling album.

After their next album, ***Just Because,*** the following year, Sherman and Terry left the group. They were the driving force behind the contemporary sound of The Imperials and their departure left a big hole. But we soon discovered that Armond and Jim had a lot of gas left in the tank. Russ Taff and Dave Will soon rounded out the quartet. We were more than ready to take a chance with the "new" Imperials.

Signing The Imperials created a challenge. As a CCM group with a Southern gospel history, they just didn't fit well with our growing contemporary Myrrh label, our traditional Word label or our Southern gospel Canaan label. So we formed Dayspring label just for the Imperials. It ultimately became home to other great artists as well, including First Call, Kenny Marks, Wayne Watson and Morris Chapman.

Gary S. Paxton had produced the two successful contemporary Imperial albums for Benson, so we contracted him to produce their first album for us in a decision that didn't work out very well.

We advanced $35,000 (a big recording budget for that time) to Gary and he delivered what we hoped was another hit album. I sat in my Word office with Roland Lundy, Dan Johnson and Buddy Huey (our new V.P. of A&R) preparing to play the master tape on a 15 IPS reel-to-reel player. Our anticipation was high, but the hit songs we hoped for just weren't there.

DID YOU KNOW?

Originally known as "Jake Hess and the Imperials," the group recorded with Elvis Presley from 1966 to 1971. Elvis was a fan of gospel music and Jake Hess specifically. Ultimately a young bass singer named Armond Morales and tenor Jim Murray would guide The Imperials from Southern gospel stardom into Contemporary Christian Music history.

The first Imperials record for Word had to be a huge success. Period. Our reputation (and $35,000) was on the line. As the last song on the tape came to an end, I rewound it and put it back in the 12" square box. I looked at the guys and said, "No one will ever hear this record." I promptly put that

THE "LOST" IMPERIALS ALBUM

Thirty years later Word decided to release that album and entitled it The Lost Album. It wasn't lost at all. I knew exactly where it was!

box under my desk. It remained there under my feet for the next five years.

The next day I called Chris Christian, explained the situation, and asked if he could produce a new Imperials recording for us in the next six weeks. We didn't have an emergency planning meeting or conduct a focus group to solve this problem. I just called my new friend and colleague—the one producer I absolutely knew would deliver a quality album.

SAILING AHEAD

Our very first Imperials album was called ***Sail On***, and it completed their musical transformation from gospel quartet to a Contemporary Christian Music powerhouse. ***Sail On*** sold over 300,000 copies. So The Imperials went from selling 50,000 albums at Benson to 300,000 for us at Word, while

◀ Russ Taff explaining to Chris Christian & Stan Moser how he remembered his lines at the Dove Awards.

replacing half the group! That was a huge success, and in the process we were all introduced to a young singer named Russ Taff who was destined for CCM greatness.

In 1978, Chris produced the second Imperials album for Dayspring, ***Heed The Call***. It sold better than ***Sail On***. ***Heed the Call*** featured the classic song "O Buddha." It also included "Praise The Lord," which was co-written by Brown Bannister and Michael Hudson. The Imperials CCM career was soaring.

Chris recalls the first time he heard the final mix of "Praise the Lord" in the studio. "We finished the song at 4:30 AM, and Brown and I just sat there, not saying a word, for what felt like 10 minutes. It was a deeply spiritual moment. It was as if God was in the control room saying, 'Be still.' Finally I looked at Brown and said, 'This song will be around long after we are gone.'" I suspect he is right about that.

From Andrae and Evie, to the Imperials and Second Chapter of Acts. From the Talbot Brothers and Keith Green to Dallas Holm's "Rise Again" and Chuck Girard's "Sometimes Alleluia," Contemporary Christian Music was in the midst of explosive growth.

Little did I know that our world would soon be rocked by a humble teenage girl from Nashville. I was about to receive a phone call that would send the entire industry into the stratosphere.

MORE ABOUT... *SAIL ON*

While listening to the Imperials hit song "No Shortage," Chris Christian remarked to a friend that he could write a better song in five minutes. At the time, he was sitting on a beach in Clearwater, Florida. As Chris watched some sailboats drift by, "Sail On" jumped out of his "inner songwriter" and onto that pad of paper. He heard the words and melody completely in his head. Five minutes later the song was done.

▲ From Top Left: Petra, Michael Omartian, Keith Green, Steve Green, Chris Christian, White Heart & Dick Clark

THE TIMES THEY ARE A CHANGIN'

1976 –1984

Chapter 8

WHAT A DIFFERENCE YOU'VE MADE

Between 1974 and 1976 our record sales at Word had more than doubled. And they would double again over the next two years thanks in part to a phone call from Chris Christian. After our success with B.J. Thomas, I had quickly initiated a distribution and marketing agreement between Chris and Word that allowed Chris to sign new artists to his production company (Home Sweet Home Productions) and release their albums through our Myrrh label. That deal was about to pay big dividends for Word.

Chris got right to the point. "Hey I just signed the first artist to Home Sweet Home; I think she could be the first artist for our new distribution deal. She's only 16, but she is really good. I've got a couple of demos (songs) I could send you." Obviously, the only way to send the demos in those days was by mail. That whole process would take a week.

I was busy and of course very important—in my own mind. So I quickly said, "Just play me what you have." Chris paused, "Over the phone?" I said, "Sure. Just hold the phone up to the speaker."

When the second song was finished, Chris asked what I thought. I said, "Sounds good. How long will it take to get her record done?"

I had just heard the first songs from the artist who would revolutionize Contemporary Christian Music—and I didn't have a clue. It was just another record to me, but God clearly had His hand on Amy Grant.

The spiritual root of Amy's family ran deep. She attended Belmont Church, which was experiencing true revival under Pastor Don Finto. Brown Bannister served in the student ministry at Belmont. After playing a few of her songs for Brown, Amy asked him if he would help her record them for her family and friends. Brown had no idea at the time that he was helping to lay the foundation for what would become his most successful collaborative project. It was that cassette that Brown played for his friend Chris—and Brown listened in the day Chris played the demos over the phone for me.

It is interesting that Chris, Brown and Amy all grew up in the Church of Christ, where musical instruments were not used. Yet they all helped bring a new kind of Christian music to millions.

A karaoke moment for Brown Banister, Amy Grant and her sisters, Carol Nuismer, Kathy Harrell and Mimi Verner.
Courtesy of Brown Bannister

Chris and Brown produced Amy's first album, and then Chris turned production over to Brown who would work with Amy on many more. Over the next decade, I would help deliver eight Amy Grant albums to her fans and had the joy of watching this 16-year-old Tennessee girl mature into one of the most celebrated artists of our lifetime. Amy repackaged truth for a generation of listeners and inspired many young girls to give their musical talent to the Lord.

THE CHANGING OF THE GUARD

While Amy would soon lead the CCM parade at Word, sales of Andrae Crouch and Evie records were still paying the bills. Roland, Dan Johnson and I really enjoyed being around Andrae Crouch. He was quick-witted and endlessly creative.

His songs, "The Blood Will Never Lose its Power," "My Tribute," "Through It All," "Jesus Is The Answer" and so many others touched millions and are vital contributions to the great American CCM songbook. Andrae Crouch will always be the first iconic figure on the CCM stage in my book.

Evie's charisma, warmth and love flowed freely on stage and off it. She was one of the best communicators

MORE ABOUT ... BROWN BANNISTER

As a college student at Abilene Christian College, Brown Bannister planned on being a doctor. But when his college friend Chris Christian invited him to Nashville to play in his Opryland Theme Park bluegrass band, Brown's heart was "completely captured" by Jesus during a visit to Belmont Church on Music Row.

Eventually becoming a ministry leader for the church, Bannister and his group Homecoming often played at the Koininia coffee shop next to Belmont Church. Koininia served as a concert venue for many Christian artists such as Don Francisco, Nancy Honeytree and Randy Matthews.

Initially working under Chris Christian's tutelage, Brown became a successful engineer, producer and songwriter. In 2014 he was inducted into the Gospel Music Hall of Fame. His producer credits include Amy Grant, David Meece, The Imperials, Debbie Boone, Michael English, Petra, Steven Curtis Chapman and CeCe Winans and many others.

I've ever heard. Her peak as an artist came with the release of ***Mirror*** in 1977. By that time we had rallied all of the resources of Word behind her, and the results were astounding. Evie stepped on stages from America to Europe and Australia, winning everyone's heart along the way. She may have been, as she often sang, only "four-foot-eleven and going to heaven," but the 17-year-old singing phenomenon became a 20-year-old recording star with the Gold Records to prove it.

Then as her career and record sales rocketed, Evie made a decision that changed the landscape of Contemporary Christian Music—she married a dynamic young pastor from Sweden named Pelle Karlsson. Soon it became clear that the Evie era of CCM was coming to an end, and that meant a huge sales problem for us.

Seventeen thousand people attended her final major concert in Minneapolis in 1980. When the concert ended, she simply walked off the center stage of Contemporary Christian Music. And she never came back.

At the peak of Evie's career in 1977, my life was a mess. I had very little relationship with Christ, and she knew it. After one of her concerts, she gave me a "just released" copy of the New International Version New Testament. I will always be grateful for the way God used Evie to push me closer and closer to surrendering my life to Jesus. Evie and Andrae—two amazing people and talented communicators— created a pathway for the ministries, careers and livelihoods of so many of us. I'm not sure, but it may have been necessary for them both to step aside to make room for the next wave of talented and called singers and musicians who were ready to join the CCM explosion at Word, Sparrow and Benson.

However, I am certain of this: God used Andrae Crouch and Evie Tornquist to deliver some amazing music and the life-changing message of Jesus to millions who needed hope in their lives—including me.

Chapter 9

THE SPIRIT MOVES

In 1977, Greg Nelson was just another youth director at a small church in Bismarck, North Dakota. From the moment he heard Ronn Huff's arrangements on the album *Alleluia*, Greg dreamed of becoming a professional arranger and producer of great music for the church, and he planned to create a record label to make great Christian music.

In pursuit of his dream, Greg convinced five local sponsors to invest $15,000 each into his new company, Spirit Records. The only problem was he had no artists to record and no way to promote an album even if he did.

Greg loved what was happening at Sparrow Records, so he called Billy Ray Hearn for 30 straight days before finally getting a response. Billy Ray had the artists and the sales team needed for Greg's newfound Spirit label, and in early 1978 Greg and his wife, Pam, moved to California to work for Sparrow Publishing and build Spirit Records.

FORGIVE US OUR DEBTS

Just two short years later, Spirit Records had released albums by Benny Hester and Albrecht, Roley and Moore, but the albums did not sell very well. When retailers began returning the unsold product, Greg and his label suddenly owed Sparrow $76,000 for those excess returns.

Greg's dream seemed to come crashing down. Spirit Records was out of money and he soon took a job with another California publishing company when they decided to acquire what was left of Spirit Records.

Greg wasn't the first or last brilliant and creative musician to find that running a record label took a different set of skills. Of course, he was devastated. However, he never lost his passion for arranging and producing. When John Thompson called from Nashville and asked Greg to write string arrangements for a Sharalee Lucas album in early 1980, he was ready to go.

Unfortunately, when Greg arrived in Nashville to work on the charts, he found those arrangements had been written

MORE ABOUT...DAN BROCK

Dan Brock began his career in CCM as a student at the University of the Cumberlands in Eastern Kentucky promoting concerts for artists like Randy Matthews, Honeytree and Petra. In 1976, he moved to Nashville to join Joe Moscheo's booking and management company, New Direction Artists Guild.

Dan began managing Randy, Petra and Steve Camp before merging with Ray Nenow's company to create the T.A.M.E. Agency in 1977. Their combined artist roster included Amy Grant, Benny Hester, Farrell and Farrell, Chris Christian and John Michael Talbot.

by someone else. Devastated once again, with his wife and young daughter still living in California, and still in debt to Sparrow, Greg crashed on the floor of an apartment that Ray Nenow and Dan Brock shared.

Greg needed a break, and Billy Ray was the first to offer real help. When he heard that Greg had moved to Nashville, he forgave the $76,000 debt. Then he added, "But if you find an artist or two in Nashville that I should hear, do let me know." That decision set Greg free from debt and brought Sparrow Records two of its most successful artists just a few years down the road.

Greg cried out to God one more time, and that was the beginning of the most miraculous two weeks of Greg's life. It all started when Ray Nenow learned that Joe English (drummer for Paul McCartney and Wings) wanted to record for Ray's Refuge Records. Greg was Ray's first choice to produce that album.

Before producing Joe English, Ray knew Greg needed to become an affiliate with ASCAP, BMI or SESAC. So he took Greg to meet a former piano player for the Imperials and his former boss at New Direction Artists Guild, Joe

MORE ABOUT... BILL GATHER

Bill Gaither started the Bill Gaither Trio in 1956 with his siblings Danny and Mary Ann. After Mary Ann got married, Bill's wife, Gloria, replaced her. Over the years the Bill Gaither Trio would also include Sherry Slatter, Betty Fair, Gary McSpadden and Michael English.

Bill and Gloria's best-known songs include "Because He Lives," "The King Is Coming," "Something Beautiful," "He Touched Me," "It Is Finished," "There's Something About That Name," and "Let's Just Praise The Lord." They have collectively won eight Grammy Awards and more than two dozen Dove Awards.

As Bill puts it, *"If we have done anything right over the years, I hope we have built bridges where people could connect with God and with each other. That is what started us writing and what will keep us going for the rest of our lives."*

Moscheo, who just happened to be the VP of BMI. Greg was hoping for a $200 advance by signing with BMI. But evidently God had something bigger in mind. A week later, Joe Moscheo handed Greg a check for $10,000!

That first Joe English album became an instant hit. More and more work began to flow his way, and Greg was finally able to move Pam and their daughter to Nashville. Before long he received a career-and life-altering phone call from his new friends at Benson's Impact label. They wanted to know if Greg would be interested in producing the next Sandi Patty record.

Chapter 10

HE'S ALIVE

As I said in the beginning of this book, my personal Christian Music Hall of Fame has very few members: Jarrell McCracken, Marvin Norcross, Kurt Kaiser, Ralph Carmichael, Billy Ray Hearn, Bob Benson, Bill Gaither and...Bob MacKenzie.

For many years, I didn't understand Mac (as most of his friends called him) and wasn't sure I liked him. First of all he was a Yankee, which was a big deal for a Texan like me. He was a musician's musician, and I'm a far cry from a musician. And Mac was a fierce competitor for most of my career.

Bob became the CEO of the Nashville Symphony in 1964. He left the symphony in 1966 and went to the Benson Company where he produced most of the recordings that Benson sold for the next decade. I don't know how a symphony conductor could produce Southern gospel hits, but Mac did. He invaded that traditional "four male voices and a piano" world and added symphonic elements that drove the Southern gospel genre and traditional church music in new directions. He was also one of the driving forces behind the contemporary explosion for Reba Rambo, The Imperials and Andrus, Blackwood and

Company at Benson.

After arriving at Benson, Mac and Bill Gaither became friends and created several projects for Benson's Heartwarming label. In 1973, Mac suggested to Bill that they could combine the Trio's unique song and story format for church choirs around the country. They worked with arranger Ronn Huff to create an album and choral book that would incorporate personal testimonies and arrangements (choir and orchestra) of Gaither songs. The result was the first Recording Industry Association of America (RIAA) Gold Record in the history of Christian music.

DID YOU KNOW?

Ronn Huff and Bob MacKenzie both began their music careers at RCA studios in the 1960's. According to Bill Gaither, "A lot of people heard our music only because of Ronn Huff's involvement."

In 1976, the Gaither and MacKenzie families vacationed together on Nantucket Island. One afternoon while Mac and Bill floated in the pool, Bill suddenly asked Mac, "Have you ever considered starting a new venture that is totally focused on making the music that you discover rather than artists that you have inherited?"

That question hit a nerve with Mac. Less than a year later, he left Benson and started the Paragon label for more traditional church recordings and created a partnership with Gary Paxton for Gary's upstart contemporary New Pax record label. In my position as head of all sales and marketing for Word, I wanted to distribute anything Bob MacKenzie produced. His string of successful recordings at Benson was too big to ignore.

Mac seemed suspicious of my efforts. After all, I was the one leading the charge against him for years. But I don't know that he had much of a choice other than Word. Benson was probably not all that interested in selling his Paragon or NewPax product. We were the best alternative.

Mac was well known for his surprising creativity, his wit and his unique approach to life. He seemed driven to perfection and success in every venture he undertook, whether that was recording an album or building a company.

Shortly after signing our new distribution contract, I flew to Nashville to meet Mac in an old house on 18th Avenue just off Music Row. For some reason, Mac brought the founder of NewPax Records, Gary S. Paxton, to the meeting.

Gary walked in wearing a lime green jumpsuit, carrying a giant bottle of Sprite and sporting a strange haircut that never could have made it to the pages of GQ. He talked fast and seemed easily distracted, and at the time, I had no idea about his unusual success as an artist and producer. I wasn't quite sure what Mac saw in Gary, but when Gary intro-

MORE ABOUT... GARY PAXTON

Gary Paxton began his music career in 1959 with the million-selling Top 40 radio single, "It Was I." Over the next few years he worked with artists like The Association, Paul Revere & the Raiders, The Four Freshmen and Tommy Roe among many others.

Gary is best known for his involvement in two novelty hits: The 1960 No. 1 smash "Alley Oop" — written by Dallas Frazier but recorded by Gary's The Hollywood Argyles — and a 1962 No. 1 hit inspired by the Mashed Potato dance craze, "Monster Mash," which Paxton produced and recorded with its author Bobby "Boris" Pickett.

duced me to NewPax' first recording artist, it all made sense. That artist was Don Francisco.

ANOTHER BROTHER OF THE SON

Don Francisco was and is one of the most gifted musical storytellers ever heard, but when Gary Paxton introduced us in 1976, he seemed to me to be another hippie who didn't trust anyone—particularly me.

Like many other musicians, Don had moved to Nashville to pursue his music career. From the time he was a teenager, he wanted to be a recording artist. Then he met the Lord. And as he told me, "When God revealed Himself to me I finally had something to sing about!"

While attending Belmont College just off Music Row, Don was given an opportunity to record a demo. He was pursuing his dream, and Don was about to see God direct his path in a most unexpected way.

One day in early 1975, as he drove down Music Row (16th Avenue) toward downtown Nashville, Don noticed a sign on Belmont Church: "Men's Prayer Meeting, 7 AM, Monday." He had never set foot in Belmont Church and sure didn't make a habit of getting up at 7 AM. But for some reason he showed up for that prayer meeting on Monday morning.

A man wearing a maroon jump suit and cowboy boots with pointed brass toes introduced himself to Don as Gary Paxton. Don soon found out that Gary was a music producer, and one of the only producers in town making Contemporary Christian recordings. Don later gave him his demo cassette.

Soon after, Gary signed Don to the NewPax label. Don's first album, ***Brother of the Son***, didn't sell well. When Gary left Nashville a year later, Don was free to sign a new contract with

Bob MacKenzie, who had taken over the NewPax label.

The second Don Francisco album for NewPax was called ***Forgiven***. Why Mac didn't call it ***He's Alive*** is a mystery to me today. That one song introduced Don to millions.

Don wrote "He's Alive" in a Nashville duplex while attending Donelson Bible Chapel. He had intended to write a song about Jesus' resurrection from Thomas' point of view, moving the listener from doubt to faith. But as he worked on the song, Don realized that he identified more with Peter. He felt he had failed or betrayed Jesus so many times in his own life. Three weeks later, he played his original version of "He's Alive" for his wife. That version ended without the final chorus. She reacted, "What? You can't stop there like that! It isn't finished." Half an hour later one of the greatest songs in CCM history *was* finished.

Now remember, Bill Gaither was Mac's business partner in Paragon/NewPax, and Bill had the largest platform of any artist in Christian music at the time. He made sure that the entire church world heard "He's Alive." Bill knew that his audience would be shocked to see a hippie like Don Francisco walk onto his stage carrying a guitar.

© CCMMagazine.com

So Bill always put his arm around Don and set him up to win the hearts of the audience. Then Don's awesome performance of "He's Alive" sealed the deal—every time.

Mac used his time at Paragon/NewPax to launch many other well-known artists including Farrell and Farrell, Truth, and Debby Boone's solo Christian recordings—all while trying to manage the Bill Gaither Trio. Of course his life was chaotic. But that was the norm for Bob MacKenzie!

A NEW BENSON COMPANY

By 1979, Paragon/NewPax had successfully produced a lot of powerful CCM music but had also managed to lose a lot of Bill Gaither's investment capital. It was time to change strategy.

Zondervan Publishing was one of the leading book and Bible publishers in the world. Headquartered in Grand Rapids, Michigan, they owned dozens of successful retail stores across the country. They also had a choral music division called Singspiration and a small record label, Milk and Honey Records.

Zondervan had recently purchased the Benson Company, but Bob Benson had passed away, and there was no one to champion the creative side of that company. Before long, the logical choice seemed to be to bring in Bob MacKenzie and his friend and chief operations officer at Paragon, Wayne Erickson.

Paragon/NewPax entered into an agreement with Zondervan to merge their assets with The Benson Company and put Mac at the helm. Suddenly, the sleeping giant at Benson woke up, and Word and Sparrow had a serious new competitor to deal with. Naturally the New Benson Company quickly moved the distribution of Paragon/NewPax from

Word to Benson when our contract expired.

During the three years we partnered with Paragon, I never did understand Bob MacKenzie. We lived in two different worlds. He was constantly innovating while I was always trying to catch up and please him with our sales numbers. He wasn't impressed. When Mac took over The New Benson we became intense competitors once again.

Mac's years at the Benson Company were chaotic. He helped launch artists like Sandi Patty and Larnelle Harris, and Benson made significant sales inroads into Contemporary Christian Music, but he just wasn't good at managing cash or corporate expectations. Things were so bad that Zondervan executives demanded a "come to Jesus" meeting in late 1982. The night before that meeting, Bob suffered a heart attack at the Benson office. The wheels had come off the dream. Just one year later Bob MacKenzie left the New Benson Company he had helped create.

A VOLVO, A MOWER AND A GOLD RECORD

Those who worked closely with Bob MacKenzie regularly encountered his unique combination of musical genius and tendency to quickly change direction and focus. There are countless stories about Mac's unique personality. But to me, one story paints a perfect picture of the Bob MacKenzie we all got to know and learned to love.

In the early 1970's, arranger Ronn Huff and his wife Donna had become close friends with Bob and Joy MacKenzie. The two couples also lived in the same neighborhood. As neighbors will sometimes do, Bob and Ronn bought a lawn mower together.

One day, needing to mow his lawn, Ronn dropped by the

MacKenzie house. He found that Mac was out of town and the mower was missing. Joy told him that the mower was likely in the back of their old Volvo that Mac drove to the airport. So Ronn drove to the Nashville Airport and cruised through the parking areas until he saw a mower sticking out the trunk of a car.

Sure enough, he found his mower. But as he pulled the mower from the old Volvo, Ronn found something else. Sitting right in the midst of trunk debris was the master tape of ***Alleluia: A Praise Gathering,*** the soon-to-be-released first-ever RIAA Gold Record in the history of Christian music.

That's a perfect picture of the Bob MacKenzie so many of us learned to love. Making the music that would impact millions was already done. And he was off to work on the next big thing. Fortunately for us all, Ronn picked a good day to mow his yard.

SWALLOWED UP BY LIFE

Early in this book, I wrote that "Life is designed to be lived *together* in harmony with people you love, admire and trust, even if it takes years to arrive at each of those conclusions." Bob MacKenzie is one of several people I had in mind when I wrote that sentence. We'll continue the chronology of events that shaped the CCM Industry in the next chapter, but I want to insert "the rest of the Bob MacKenzie story" here.

Bob asked to see me in early 1998. It had been years since our last conversation. I listened carefully as Bob told me about his last doctor visit in New York. During a heart exam he had briefly died on the treadmill.

He knew that his time on Earth was limited and he wanted me to release Buddy Green's new album on my small record label. I worked closely on Buddy's new album with Mac over the next few months, and I grew to love *that* Bob MacKenzie.

Around 4 PM, on October 23, 2000, Mac died while sitting in his favorite chair at home. His wife Joy was with him. She called some of his friends, including Dan and Sara Posthuma. When they arrived the house was empty except for Joy and Mac. Dan approached the body of his old friend and mentor still sitting in his chair wearing a blue velour jogging suit.

Soon the house did fill up with great old friends including John Coates, Buddy Greene, Dann Huff and many more. John began to play the piano and the concert of Mac's dream was in full force. They spent the next five hours celebrating and

▼ Life in the studio with the Bill Gaither Trio.
Gary McSpadden, Gloria Gaither, Wayne Erickson, Stan Moser, Bill Gaither, Bob MacKenzie

remembering the life of Bob MacKenzie—while his body sat right where his spirit had been swallowed up by life.

▲ Bob MacKenzie
1938-2000
Courtesy Dan & Sara Posthuma

At one point, Joy walked past the master bedroom and noticed the door was closed. She knocked on her own bedroom door. Dan Posthuma was in there with five other friends. He quickly responded to the puzzled look on Joy's face, "We'd like to plan Bob's memorial service if that is okay with you." Of course it was all right with Joy. Mac was the consummate event guy and these were his protégées.

At 9:30 PM, five and a half hours after Mac's death, Dan suggested to Joy it was time to call someone to remove the body. She agreed and the celebration came to an end for that night.

The great vision and passion Bob MacKenzie imparted to artists, songwriters and executives lives on today through the lives of so many. His creativity, wit and determination to produce the finest expression of God's love and grace that we can muster will never die.

Chapter 11

GOTTA TELL SOMEBODY

I want you to imagine a prehistoric time. A long-ago time when there was no social media, no Internet and no satellite radio. No MySpace, Facebook, Instagram, YouTube, Twitter or whatever else has been invented as you read this book. It was a place where the "dinosaurs" of 33 1/3 and 45-rpm records, eight-tracks, and cassette tapes roamed through "record stores."

That's where we lived in those ancient days of the mid 1970's. Contemporary Christian Music was exploding, and we were running as fast as we could to tell the story, but the media options were limited by today's standards.

We were on a mission to sell great music, but we faced serious barriers to getting the music out to the public. We depended upon success with a small number of progressive (for that day) radio stations, some locally owned Bible bookstores and a few articles in some print magazines.

Most Christian radio stations played preachers, Black gospel (as it was called at the time) and Southern gospel music. In fact, our greatest success with our Southern gospel label, Canaan Records, came from local radio hosts who bought

Sunday morning time slots on their local stations as a personal ministry effort.

Most Christian radio stations and networks of that era just didn't understand this new Contemporary Christian Music. Christian television was also skeptical. Even the most progressive Christian bookstores were reluctant to promote Contemporary Christian Music...until the music began to sell. Yes, Christian *Book*stores. The very name captures the hurdle we faced.

Many stores weren't even equipped to display records. So our greatest marketing tool was providing album display fixtures of all sizes and shapes to Christian retailers. Surely you remember what it was like to go by your favorite store and flip through an album bin.

We did get some coverage in magazines like *Christianity Today*, *Moody Monthly*, *Campus Life*, *Charisma* and *Christian Life*, but they reached a more traditional church audience. At Word, Sparrow and Benson we did all we could to expand the impact of Contemporary Christian Music, but reaching our potential audience depended on God providing new visionary leaders in radio, television, retail and print media.

TURN UP THE RADIO

Jim Willems was one of those visionary leaders. When I first met Jim, I knew him as the owner of Maranatha Village, one of our most important Christian retail stores. He was smart enough to put his store on the same block as Calvary Chapel in Costa Mesa, California. Maranatha Village quickly became the leading retailer in our marketplace, but Jim understood the need to combine retail with radio and print publications in order to drive the market.

JOHN STYLL © CCMMagazine.com

In 1974, Jim made a bold move. He bought an hour of air time during drive time each day on local station KGER and hired a young man named John Styll to create and host a show featuring Christian music. And Jim wasn't finished taking chances. That show was broadcast live from Maranatha Village.

John was fully aware of the exploding impact of Jesus Music in his area, but the music was still very controversial in the mainstream church. Before long, they moved their program to KMAX FM.

John's new KMAX program was four hours long and included a wide spectrum of Christian music—everything from the Bill Gaither Trio to Barry McGuire, Evie, Andrae Crouch and Second Chapter of Acts. As John said, "It sure wasn't Christian rock, but we did push the edges from time to time."

Radio was alive and well in Jim's retail store and new customers appeared daily, but Jim's vision wasn't complete. He bought a very small Orange County Christian newspaper called *The Golden Coast Good News.*

He quickly changed the name to *Contemporary Christian Acts,* and put John Styll in charge of the music section of the newspaper.

By the middle of 1978, John and Jim were ready to launch

MORE ABOUT... K-LOVE

Bob Anthony, a popular radio personality from the San Francisco area was the founder of KCLB in Santa Rosa, California, which signed on the air in 1982 and would be the seed that eventually grew into the K-LOVE Radio Network. The first song Bob played on that station was Praise the Lord from the Imperials. So the Imperials launched what would become the largest CCM radio network in the world.

In 1986 Dick Jenkins was hired as General Manager and He added consultant Brad Burkhart who helped bring the vision and drive to expand K-LOVE'S reach throughout the U. S. for the next two decades. David Pierce, Jon Rivers, and current President & CEO Mike Novak all joined K-LOVE during that time, and since then K-LOVE has grown to a weekly audience more than 14,000,000 listeners. K-LOVE's Positive Encouraging content impacts lives for Christ every day, it's amazing what God has done.

a new magazine devoted to Contemporary Christian Music. They designed it to reach the growing number of industry executives and retailers who promoted contemporary music. The record labels didn't immediately warm to the idea, but John and Jim moved forward. The first issue of *Contemporary Christian Music Magazine*, released in July of 1978, featured The Boone Girls (Debby and sisters) on the cover.

With the magazine, Christian radio and sales charts had a home, and retailers had a way to evaluate what al bums they would put on their shelves. Of course, the traditionalists barked, "You shouldn't be ranking Christian songs!"

It didn't take long for John and Jim to recognize that the demand for their magazine extended far beyond industry execs and retailers. Consumers wanted to read their magazine too. So they re-worked their editorial approach and began to serve radio, retail and consumers equally. John had a big hit on his hands, and those of us at Word, Sparrow and Benson soon realized we had a great new marketing tool to exploit. And we did.

John Styll and Jim Willems weren't the only ones combining Christian broadcasting and publications. Nearly 3,000 miles away in New Jersey, another young man named Joe Battaglia started his own Christian magazine, *Alternatives*. Joe quickly followed the release of his magazine by hosting a Christian-focused TV talk show on cable Channel 54 in West Orange, New Jersey. When WWDJ, one of the top pop radio stations in New York, switched its format to Christian music in 1974, Joe did a story on the switch in his magazine, and the manager at WWDJ hired Joe as their "token Christian sales person."

Three years later, Joe began searching the greater New York area for a concert hall or theater to produce WWDJ's first Contemporary Christian Music live event. He decided to hold it in a place that really needed the Gospel—an adult theater in Passaic, New Jersey!

That first concert was a huge success. On October 1, 1977, more than 2,000 people came to hear Phil Keaggy and the Love Inn Band (featuring future CCM leaders Peter York, Lynn Nichols and Phil Madeira). The adult theater manager thought WWDJ still played rock music, and a concert with "the Love Inn Band" made sense to him. Obviously, he was shocked when he had to take down all the pictures of nude women and replace them with pictures of a Christian band.

That first concert was so successful that just five months later the station brought Keith Green to perform, and WWDJ broadcasted the concert live to the entire New York City metro area. Less than one year later, Joe and WWDJ found themselves at the Meadowlands, home of the New York Giants and New York Jets football teams. They stood in the middle of more than 50,000 believers and reached out to the area with great Christian speakers and Andrae Crouch at what was called the "Jesus '78" rally.

By this time, Joe had become a fixture at an event called the National Gospel Radio Seminar. NGRS (as it became known) had been started in 1972 as a place for mostly Southern gospel stations to share ideas. During Joe's first NGRS, he recalls sitting in a room with about 20 other guys (including John Styll), "talking about music that had no name and a format that had no definition." Contemporary Christian radio simply didn't exist at the time, but that was about to change rapidly.

Stations like KXOJ in Tulsa, and KBHL in Lincoln, Nebraska soon joined the Contemporary Christian Music explosion. When KYMS in Santa Ana, California, added a show that featured Jon Rivers to their programming, the CCM radio revolution was off and running across the country.

Joe's success at WWDJ caught the attention of Dave Swanson, owner of a small station, WLIX, on Long Island. WLIX had fallen on tough times but Dave wasn't ready to give up. Instead, he offered half of the station to Joe. Based on a page-and-a-half contract and a handshake, Joe turned WLIX into one of the great stations in the CCM radio explosion. Joe hired Lloyd Parker as his Program Director. Lloyd went on to help build K-LOVE, today's largest Christian Music network.

GROWING PAINS

As with every "revolution," the CCM wave hit some serious challenges. Leaders in the Southern gospel music world had founded both the National Gospel Radio Seminar and the Gospel Music Association. Needless to say, CCM didn't fit well with the GMA board members and certainly not with the

Dove Awards.

The Gospel Music Association had launched The Dove Awards in 1969 to honor the best Southern gospel groups and songs every year. I still remember my first experience at The Dove Awards in 1971 at Nashville's War Memorial Auditorium. The Blackwood Brothers, one of the all-time great Southern gospel groups, won 11 out of the 12 awards that night. Their fans came out in force to vote for their favorite group. That Dove Awards was expunged from the record book, and new voting regulations were implemented.

My role as head of sales at Word meant selling all kinds of gospel music—from CCM to Southern gospel, church musicals, and what we called Black gospel at the time. By 1978

MORE ABOUT...PAUL BAKER

PAUL BAKER (REAL NAME: FRANK EDMONDSON) WAS ONE OF THE FIRST ON-AIR CCM RADIO PERSONALITIES. His journey began in the late 1960s when he was stationed in Belgium with the Army. As a subscriber to Word's Family Record Club, he was introduced to artists like the Spurrlows and The Young and Free. Not exactly today's CCM, but Frank was hooked. By 1972, out of the Army and living in Tampa, Frank launched a radio program called "A Joyful Noise." Before long, he was playing artists like Larry Norman and other CCM artists in Tampa and then in Wichita, Kansas, where he moved a few months later.

I found myself on the board of the Gospel Music Association right in the middle of a changing of the guard. That allowed me to watch real grace and honor in practice as those legendary founders of the GMA began to embrace their Contemporary Christian Music counterparts.

I'm not sure the overall GMA establishment really knew what to do with this new music or us. But it became clear that Marvin Norcross and Bob Benson were clearing the way for us behind the scenes. And we will all be forever grateful for Don Butler. He really helped build a bridge between the "old" and the "new" GMA.

As more and more Christian radio stations began to embrace Contemporary Christian Music, we began to meet regularly with those contemporary radio pioneers like Joe Battaglia, Paul Baker and Lloyd Parker as part of our marketing strategies.

As the CCM radio audience grew, Contemporary Christian concert venues began to emerge. In addition to Nashville's Koinonia Coffee House, The Lamb's Club in New York City became another hotspot for Christian artists.

More and more local Christian bookstores embraced the music as well. So many stores and their owners, managers and employees became real promoters of the music. They included Dan Jantz at Fresno Book House, Lloyd Johnson of Better Bookroom in Wichita, Chuck Wallington at Christian Supply in Spartanburg, South Carolina, Steve Potratz at Parable Book Store in San Luis Obispo, California, Mart Green at Mardel's in Oklahoma City and Les Dietzman with the Family Book Stores. Thanks to their vision, Contemporary Christian Music reached millions of retail shoppers across the country.

AS SEEN ON TV

As CCM popularity grew, the momentum carried into the Gospel Music Association. Gospel Music Week was one of the best GMA achievements. Beginning in 1980, this event in Nashville brought key radio, retail and label people together with fans and the artists. It was just a lot of fun in the early days.

The GMA Week became home to the Dove Awards. Television became a driving force for CCM when the 1984 Dove Awards were televised on CBN.

Television visibility created a whole new marketing opportunity. The MTV revolution was in full force with pop music, and two talented young men in California would soon follow that lead and make history with a weekly television show called ***Real Videos***.

In 1983, Jim Hodson was a popular drive time DJ for Southern California's top CCM music station KYMS. He was also a volunteer cameraman at Trinity Broadcast Network's rapidly expanding television ministry.

When Jim went to Matt Crouch, son of TBN founders Paul and Jan Crouch, with the idea for ***Real Videos***, Matt was immediately interested, but wisely skeptical. In his words, "We were

MORE ABOUT... SALES AROUND THE WORLD

Sales of our albums were not limited to Christian retailers in the United States. Thanks to visionary men like Ian Hamilton in the UK, Gerry Scott, Jim Sturgeon and Steve Nicolle in Canada, Stan Moulton, Norm Moulton and David Smallbone in Australia, John Muys and Alan Kennedy in New Zealand, and Johnny Sy in the Philippines, Contemporary Christian Music reached new fans far beyond our borders.

And we will be forever grateful for Ted Bleymaier in our lives. Ted began his career at Maranatha!Music with his friend Chuck Fromm, but in 1982 he joined us at Word as our VP of International Distribution. Ted's relentless passion for taking the life-changing message of Contemporary Christian Music around the world was a constant reminder to dream far beyond the weekly radio and sales charts here in the US.

about to launch a television show with no budget that could be off the air in two seconds if one too many faithful in the TBN audience complained to the right person!"

Of course, those concerns didn't stop Jim and Matt. Their very first show was soon shot on Hollywood Boulevard right in front of the world-famous Grauman's Chinese Theatre—without a city permit, of course.

Real Videos would go on to deliver nearly 400 programs over the next ten years and expose artists like Mylon and Broken Heart, Bash and the Code, Steve Taylor, Kenny Marks, Stryper, Sheila Walsh and The Allies to millions of new fans including the entire Armed Services Television Network around the world. And in the process, Matt and his team produced more than 40 song concept videos.

AND THE AWARD GOES TO...

The momentum of those years required every executive at every label to spend every day in competition for the best artists and the best positioning on radio, in store fixtures and on highly viewed television programs like ***Praise the Lord*** at TBN and ***The 700 Club*** on CBN. And, of course, we had to score plenty of visibility at the Dove Awards.

Although we were all highly competitive, GMA Week became our once-a-year opportunity to work together for the common good of all labels, and we did. The Gospel Music Association, as a neutral entity, made all that possible. We stood together for that week, and it was a lot of fun.

At Word, we left no marketing stone unturned. We even created our own National Press Day and brought writers and editors of print publications to Waco and/or Dallas. This was our opportunity to connect up-and-coming artists with dozens of editors and writers who reached thousands through magazines like ***Christianity Today***, ***Charisma***, ***Campus Life***, ***Christian Life***, ***Moody Monthly***, and of course ***CCM Magazine***.

We always looked for any creative way to connect with the establishment church audience. Radio and retail were getting on board. Even some mainstream publications were giving us coverage, but we needed "a trusted voice" to help penetrate the more traditional church audience with CCM. His name was Bill Gaither.

Bill, always a brilliant showman, became the "Ed Sullivan" of our industry. His platform instincts were formed through hard work and plain old courage. He quickly discovered that he could bring new life to the Gaither Trio platform by sharing the stage with new Contemporary Christian artists. Just ask Don Francisco. Or Steve Green. Or Amy Grant. Or Carman. Or Whiteheart. Better yet, ask Sandi Patty. In fact, you could ask any Christian music executive of that day, "How do you best expose a new artist to the largest possible audience?" One answer—"Bill Gaither."

> **DID YOU KNOW?**
>
> **The concept of the Dove Awards was originally suggested by Bill Gaither at a GMA board meeting in 1968. The idea of the award being represented by a dove is also credited to him.**

For the record, I love and admire Bill Gaither. He is in private exactly who he is in public. Bill has overcome both failure and success by his faith and the grace that comes through

Christ. He has been a driving force for decades in traditional church music (The Bill Gaither Trio/Praise Gathering), Contemporary Christian Music, and Southern gospel music. His ***Homecoming*** series of television programs and live events has reached millions.

Just a few years later, Bill would partner with Darrell Harris, Jeff Moseley and me to build the Star Song record label. As you will see a few chapters down the road, that venture worked out pretty well for all of us and some very well-known artists like Twila Paris, Newsboys, Petra, Whitecross and Phillips, Craig and Dean.

Chapter 12

I SURRENDER ALL

I kept "setting 'em up and knocking 'em down" year after year. More money. More power. More acclaim. I felt large and in charge, but I was about to meet the One who was really in charge.

In early 1977 during an Imperials concert at First Baptist Church in Waco, Jesus interrupted my outwardly successful world that was secretly filled with doubt, fear and sin. He invited me to follow Him. There was just something special about the way Dave Will, the Imperials' lead singer, presented the invitation that night. All the doubts, fears and struggles of my life suddenly paled in comparison to the hope that Dave described. In one moment, a 27-year-old overgrown, arrogant and frightened little boy finally became a forgiven child of God.

Like most children, I didn't know much about what was coming down the road, and whatever was ahead didn't matter to me. I knew I was forgiven and I had a brand-new relationship with the Lord.

I didn't walk down the aisle that night and let everyone know what had just happened. I just couldn't let those who worked for and with me know the real me. But my Southern Baptist roots demanded that I make a "public profession of faith." The only authority figure in my life at that time was my boss, Jarrell McCracken. He had trusted me with a lot of responsibilities at work, and I trusted him. The decision was easy: My profession of faith would be made across the desk from Mr. McCracken.

So at 8:30 AM on Monday morning, I walked into his office and told him what had happened to me the night before. I told the most powerful man in my life that I had finally surrendered my life to Jesus Christ. That meant my job would have to take second place.

For some reason, I honestly thought that decision would cost me my job, and I didn't really care. I had become a new creation in Christ and nothing else mattered. I actually told Jarrell that he would "probably want to replace me and I would understand that decision." He simply smiled and assured me that committing my life to Jesus was the best news he could have gotten that morning. Then in typical Jarrell fashion, he said, "Now get back to work!" I did just that, but the purpose behind everything I did at work began to slowly change.

BACK AT WORK

Our business success brought a lot of responsibility and a lot of freedom. Dan Johnson, Roland Lundy and I were a great team. If we could dream it we could do it. Thanks to our bosses at American Broadcasting, Inc., it seemed that we had unlimited resources to invest. And we had many ideas.

Naturally, the more Word grew the more attractive we became to most successful Christian artists. Soon, legendary artists (including Bill Gaither and ultimately Sandi Patty) joined the Word roster. And a lot of other labels that needed distribution and marketing services signed up with our newly formed Word Distribution division. At one point, we sold nearly 70% of all Christian music.

Our success with Evie and Andrae at Word had opened the floodgates of CCM for us. A new wave of artists including Steve Camp, David Meece and Chris Christian (as a solo artist) joined Amy Grant on our Myrrh label, and our competitors at Sparrow and Benson were growing as well.

In Nashville, The Benson Company sold hundreds of thousands of copies of Dallas Holm, Reba Rambo, Phil Johnson, Tim Sheppard and Andrus Blackwood & Company. Sparrow sales were climbing thanks to Barry McGuire, The Talbot Brothers, Second Chapter of Acts, Scott Wesley Brown and Keith Green. Customers wanted more Jesus Music *and* Contemporary Christian Music.

Many small labels sprang up all across the country including Good News (Love Song and Chuck Girard), Solid Rock (Larry Norman and Randy Stonehill), Home Sweet Home (Whiteheart, Mark Heard and Steve Archer) and Exit Records (Charlie Peacock and The 77s). As a result, we sold a lot of great music through Word Distribution that we didn't record.

After Billy Ray Hearn left Word to form Sparrow Records, Jarrell and Kurt Kaiser quickly hired a former Baptist choir director named Buddy Huey to fill the void left by Billy Ray's departure. Contemporary Christian Music was in explosive growth mode, and we were all in serious on the job training every day.

I always admired Kurt Kaiser and enjoyed working with him. He was a tremendous businessman, man of God, A&R

MORE ABOUT... MARVIN NORCROSS

When I came to Word in 1970, Marvin Norcross was the head of all operations and accounting at the company AND the founder and leader of Canaan Records (home to groups like The Happy Goodman Family, The Cathedral Quartet, Wendy Bagwell and The Sonlighters, The Florida Boys and The Inspirations).

Marvin reached out to me as a young man with no business experience and taught me how to function as an executive. He was one of the finest, most honest, dependable and trustworthy men I have ever known, and just downright fun to be around. The Lord took Marvin home through a sudden heart attack in 1980, but the 10 years we shared greatly influenced my life.

man and producer. And I truly enjoyed and admired Marvin Norcross. He was the founder of Canaan Records, our Southern gospel label. Every success we had with Southern gospel music started and ended with Marvin.

Although Buddy Huey and I came at things from different perspectives and didn't always work well together, we were part of a team with Roland Lundy (sales) and Dan Johnson (marketing) that delivered some great music to the marketplace. When I became Buddy's boss in 1979, we both realized working together wasn't an option. Buddy soon left Word and formed Priority Records (a new division of CBS Records) in Nashville.

IN A WAREHOUSE IN WACO

As the Vice President of Marketing and Sales for Word, I led the sales and marketing of all our contemporary, traditional and Southern gospel music products and our book division. Word Books published great leaders like Keith Miller, Bruce Larson and Billy Graham.

When we released Billy Graham's new book, ***The Holy Spirit***, in 1978, Billy and his right hand man, Grady Wilson, came to town to discuss marketing the book. After four hours in the conference room, we escorted Billy to the Word warehouse to speak to our employees. At 2:00 PM, Billy began speaking to about 200 workers. He opened with, "I am going to start by asking myself the question most interviewers ask me…and then I'll answer."

"'Interviewer: Dr. Graham, you've been preaching the gospel for the last 30 years. Now that you are 60 years old, what do you plan to do with the rest of your life?' Me: 'Well…30 years ago the Lord told me to go and preach the gospel. And He hasn't told me anything different since! So I guess I'll just keep on preaching the gospel.'"

Billy continued, "In fact, if you don't know Jesus Christ as your Lord and Savior, this may be your day!" In that moment, he *became* Billy Graham the evangelist, and for the next few minutes we were all confronted with the gospel message Billy had delivered to millions around the world.

His words carried great power and promise. I was standing next to a shipping table in the far corner of the room, but I was certain he was looking right at me as he spoke. Of course everyone in the room felt the same way. We were encountering the power of the Holy Spirit right then, right there, right where we worked.

Then a bell rang loudly. No, not a church bell, but the bell that signaled the afternoon coffee break broke in on the message. Billy laughed, "Well, I guess I know when it's time to quit preaching!" Then, he simply stepped down off the platform.

I often wonder what would have happened if the bell had malfunctioned that day. Would he have given an altar call? Would we have seen revival in our workplace? We will never know. But we all knew that Billy Graham lived his faith and his calling every place he went. Even in a warehouse in Waco, Texas.

A YOUNG MAN FROM ABILENE

During Buddy Huey's tenure as A&R Director, we added some great artists including Amy Grant, David Meece, Chris Christian and Steve Camp. But one of the greatest talents that Buddy brought to Word was a young man from Abilene named Michael Blanton.

Michael, an Abilene Christian University student (and friend to Chris Christian and Brown Bannister), had moved to Nashville in 1974 with the usual dream of making it in the music business. That move brought him into the ministry of Don Finto and Belmont Church, just as it did for Brown Bannister. In fact, the historic move of God at Belmont was a common bond for much of the CCM story. Pastor Don invited Michael to work at Belmont's Koinonia coffee shop; there he met some early CCM artists like Nancy Honeytree, Dogwood and Don Francisco.

Michael had landed right in the middle of the first wave of Contemporary Christian Music, but there seemed to be no way to make a living doing what he longed to do. So he moved back to Abilene and went to work for the Chamber of Commerce.

Michael thought his music career was over, but shortly after Buddy Huey came to Word as A&R Chief, he needed an assistant. Brown Bannister and Chris Christian recommended their old college friend.

It didn't take Michael long to say yes and make the move to Waco to become the Assistant A&R Director for Myrrh. And just two years later, he moved to Nashville to launch our Word office there. Nashville's Music Row was rapidly becoming a center for new CCM artists, and producers like Chris and Brown.

Matching the right producer with the right artist was always one of Michael's strengths. That's exactly what he did when he brought David Meece and Brown Bannister together to produce David's breakthrough album, ***Everybody Needs a Little Help.***

David had done two records with Myrrh at that point, but his sales didn't really warrant another record release. That is, until Mike Blanton brought Brown Bannister onboard as David's producer. The outcome? Thanks to a lot of hard work by Mike Cloer and the rest of the Myrrh radio team, the song "I Can't Believe It's True," from that album gained a lot of pop radio airplay.

David Meece's career was off and running, but the best was yet to come.

His next album, ***Are You Ready***, brought us one of the greatest CCM songs of all time, "We Are The Reason," and a national platform for David that has lasted over 30 years and reached millions.

The message here is very clear: Without great A&R leadership (remember…A&R is industry code for the executive who helps birth the great songs and recorded performances you enjoy), AND great producers (industry code for those who pick the musicians, the studio, the arrangers and capture those great performances on tapes and computers), you may never have heard your favorite song!

Over the years, I often got variations of this question: "Let's see, you don't sing, you don't play, you don't write and you don't produce music. What exactly is it that you do?" My

▼ David Meece signing his second Myrrh Records contract

© Word Music Entertainment

answer, "Well, I'm pretty good at figuring out what people do well, convincing them they do that well and getting them to work well with others. And I know a hit song when I hear one!" And my lifelong quest has been to hear another song that can really impact people.

After more than 40 years in the CCM industry, I still don't know how to make music but I sure know a lot of people who do. I'm truly amazed that I had the privilege to work with or around so many great musicians, producers, singers and artists.

Together we learned the art of making and marketing Christian music, all while learning to run a business effectively. We made plenty of mistakes along the way, but God was always right there with us, pouring out His heart through the music we sent to the millions who needed His life-changing message of hope.

MORE ABOUT... ARRANGERS

Arrangers may be best described as the musical geniuses that "take a black-and-white photograph and add vibrant color." They take a great song and create the notes that the band, orchestra and background singers deliver to each recording. That's what Ronn Huff did with the great Gaither songs of *Alleluia*.

The astounding talents of men like David Clydesdale, Don Hart, Don Wyrtzen, Larry Mayfield, Don Marsh, David Hamilton, Alan Moore, David Maddux and so many more that could be mentioned here, were often the difference between a good song and a true musical masterpiece.

Chapter 13

ONE MORE SONG FOR YOU

As I rapidly approached the end of my first decade in the Christian music industry, my days and weeks were filled with meetings, concerts, airplanes, sales reports and airplay charts.

My encounter with the Lord at the Imperials concert in Waco was very real, but the world I lived in was very real and demanding too. It takes time for a believer to become a follower, and business and my inner struggles often got in the way. But God was clearly not satisfied with second place in my life.-

Over the next few years, God used my job to direct my path right to the doorstep of godly men who would help me hear the Lord more clearly. I soon got to know Chuck Smith, John Wimber, Louis Neely and other pastors who were reaching a number of our artists and songwriters.

I could tell that the Lord was real and present to them. They seemed to actually "hear" from Him regularly and He helped them make real-time, real-life decisions. And I wanted that kind of relationship with God myself.

Over time, God continued to reach into my inner man and slowly set my life in order. I began to read the Bible and actually allow God's Word to help guide a few decisions. The process of renewing my mind was slow and painful, but I was beginning to "hear" God like Chuck, John and Louis.

A NEW ERA OF CCM

The Imperials had become the new anchor of the Contemporary Christian Music charts, and we continued to set sales records every year. There seemed to be no limit to their popularity.

Now, if you know anything about The Imperials, you realize that group has launched more than one highly successful solo Christian artist. As the Imperials began their CCM era, the group included Sherman Andrus and Terry Blackwood. But in the late 1970's, with their ***Sail On*** record, The Imperials brought us an artist whose voice and story has impacted almost every fan of Contemporary Christian Music.

IN THE STUDIO WITH RUSS TAFF & KURT KAISER.
© CCMMagazine.com

I met Russ Taff in a dressing room at the old Houston Memorial Coliseum right before an

Imperials concert. He had been part of a successful group in his hometown in Arkansas, but The Imperials were the largest stage in our industry. Appropriately he was in the men's room throwing up!

After former lead singers Terry Blackwood and Sherman Andrus left The Imperials to form Andrus Blackwood & Company, Russ was hired to sing baritone by Armond Morales and Jim Murray, who owned The Imperials at the time. Dave Will had also recently joined the group as the lead singer. Over the next few months it became very clear that Russ was far more than just a baritone singer. He had a powerful and distinct voice and a charismatic personality to match.

By the end of 1979, we were selling thousands of Imperials albums every week. Their eight-tracks, cassettes and LPs just flew off the shelves. It seemed that everyone wanted a copy of songs like "Praise The Lord" and "Oh Buddha." At the same time, The Imperials were packing out every concert, and they performed a lot of them. As a record exec, I assure you, that was not a good time to change producers. But we did.

Mike Blanton had been listening to two albums that we distributed by Word called ***Adam Again*** and ***Whitehorse*** that were performed and produced by a highly regarded LA musician named Michael Omartian. Mike approached Buddy Huey with the idea that Omartian could take the Imperials to a whole new level musically, so Buddy made the call.

Omar (as he is known to his friends) had moved to LA from Chicago as a teenager to pursue his musical dreams. Although he was raised in a Christian home, and very quickly found a home with Jack Hayford at Church on the Way, Omar did not grow up listening to church music. His passion was jazz and rock. In other words, he was a deeply committed Christian who just happened to be a world-class "secular" musician.

Omar's skill on the keyboard and his unique arranging style put him on the "A List" for many Hollywood music producers. And his access to studios gave him the opportunity to create his own albums, like the ones that had caught Mike Blanton's attention.

But Omar was in a spiritual crisis. Like many other Christians in the music business, his career success was in conflict with his walk with the Lord. As he poured his heart out to God, the Lord spoke clearly: "Quit asking Me for stuff. I want you to go to your closet every day for a month, get on your knees and praise Me." Michael knew he had heard the voice of God so that is exactly what he did—an hour a day of intimate worship time with the Lord.

As that month came to an end, Michael was asked to produce a brand-new and totally unknown pop artist named Christopher Cross. Christopher's album contained the soon-to-be hit single "Sailing," and won Grammy Awards for New Artist of the Year and Album of the Year.

That was about the same time Buddy called and asked Omar to produce a new album for The Imperials. Although he was in high demand in Hollywood, he did find time to produce the Imperials. ***One More Song For You*** only took 27 days to produce. That was all the time he could afford!

Back in the Word offices, when we heard "One More Song For You" for the first time, we knew we had found our new single. And when Omar produced the next Imperials album, ***Priority***, the group grew to an even higher musical height.

The message to the rest of the industry was quite clear: *You must find a way to make a better sound and more relevant music.* The musical genius of Michael Omartian moved the production values of Word and all Contemporary Christian Music to a new excellence. His influence on the CCM industry was similar to what Tiger Woods did for the PGA golf tour. He pushed everyone's game up to a higher gear.

This was a giant step preparing Contemporary Christian Music to compete with even the most popular radio hits, and soon we would do just that.

FROM JESUS MUSIC TO PRAISE AND WORSHIP

Michael Omartian wasn't the only one spending time praising the Lord. In 1978 I negotiated a contract with Maranatha!Music for marketing and distributing their products. They were the home to Jesus Music artists like Parable, Sweet Comfort Band, Daniel Amos, Oden Fong and the newly launched Praise Album series. That deal brought me into a long friendship with Chuck Fromm, head of Marantha at the time.

In 1978, the sales of Maranatha's Jesus Music albums were subsiding, but the Praise Albums were gaining momentum. And our new marketing and distribution deal allowed Chuck Fromm (who was Chuck Smith's nephew) to take a risk and record three new Contemporary Christian artists who were connected to Calvary Chapel: Denny Correll, Benny Hester and Leon Patillo.

I expected a growing interest in Praise Albums and some catalogue sales of Jesus Music, but I didn't realize that Maranatha would bring us two major contemporary artists of the day in Benny Hester and Leon Patillo.

I liked Leon and his wife, Jackie. It seemed that every time Leon sang and gave an altar call, dozens if not hundreds went forward. It was a very simple evangelistic message. Leon would sing his songs and at some point say, "Ok, you know it's time for you to get saved. Come on."

I grew up with Benny Hester in Waco. As a teenager, Benny had a great pop band in Central Texas called Benny and The Morticians. I had a not-so-great band called The Tidesmen. Benny was a true musician. I was more interested in attention from the girls. Of course, my plan never worked.

MARANATHA!
MUSIC®

Marantha!Music quickly became the largest-selling distributed label at Word.

Shortly after Maranatha released new albums from Leon and Benny, I received an urgent call from Chuck Fromm. He needed to see me face to face, and soon. So I flew to Orange County and found myself sitting with my new friend Chuck at the South Coast Plaza Hotel.

He faced a crisis; the Lord had told Chuck that he was taking Maranatha!Music down the wrong road. Chuck knew that Maranatha had to get back to praise and worship music and out of the CCM artist business.

He quickly assigned the contracts with Denny, Benny and Leon to our Myrrh label, and the rest is history. Benny proceeded to create two huge singles, "Nobody Knows Me Like You" with Michael Omartian and "When God Ran" with Dan Posthuma and Jeremy Smith as the producers. Leon delivered several top-selling albums and songs as well.

Marantha!Music quickly became the largest-selling distributed label at Word. God spoke. Chuck listened. Then he stepped out in faith and took action on what he heard God say. And I learned a great deal more about hearing God as I watched Chuck respond.

MORE ABOUT...WORSHIP

THE EARLY MARANATHA! PRAISE ALBUMS SET THE STAGE FOR WHAT WOULD BECOME KNOWN AS THE MODERN WORSHIP MOVEMENT. It gained new momentum in 1984 when Mike Coleman, with New Wine Magazine in Mobile, Alabama, discovered that 55,000 of their subscribers were very interested in worship.

When Don Moen and Terry Law came to Mike's home church and taught on worship, Mike caught a vision for "experiencing the manifest presence of God." Soon others like Ed Lindquist, Gerrit Gustafson and Don Moen joined with Mike in exploring this new area. They clearly saw something new. As Mike said, "We don't need another CCM company. We just want to help people find their way into God's presence."

They quickly devised a plan they called the Hosanna! Series to provide a steady flow of recorded events and new worship songs. Very quickly, 17,000 subscribers signed up to receive a new cassette tape every two months. The Hosanna Series reached out to the many church worship leaders they knew for new material. They also began recording live worship albums at major churches across the country and then around the world. Hosanna Music grew to nearly 200,000 subscribers over the next few years.

Their vision for true worship ultimately led to many great worship projects from Jack Hayford, Darlene Zschech and Hillsong, Paul Baloche and other leaders.

Chapter 14

HEED THE CALL

In 1979, as Amy's career took flight, the phone at the Grant house rang continuously. And how could you blame the magazines, radio stations and concert promoters? Amy was big news and a big concert draw already.

Amy's dad, Dr. Grant, was extremely busy with his radiology practice. He and his wife, Gloria, soon realized they needed some serious help with Amy's career. And it had to be someone they trusted completely. They found the answer sitting across from them at their dinner table.

Dan Harrell was a very successful banker in Nashville who just happened to be married to Amy's sister, Kathy. As calls to the Grant house began to pour in, Dan told Amy's mom to have all the calls referred to his office at the bank. With every new hit song on the radio, the demand for Amy's time grew more intense. It didn't take long for Dan to realize Amy needed a manager.

After meeting with a candidate or two, he came to the right conclusion: It was time to leave the security of the bank job and create Harrell and Associates to manage the never-ending list of requests for Amy's time and attention. Of course, there were no "associates" but the name sounded good to Dan.

By this time, Mike Blanton had moved to Nashville to run Word's office there, and that meant spending a lot of time working with Amy and Dan. It soon became clear to both of them that Harrell and Associates should become Blanton Harrell Management.

In April 1980, Mike left his job at Word, and Blanton Harrell Management was in business. Their management roster of artists started with Amy, and soon it was time for them to build their own record label. So they formed Reunion Records, becoming the first company in our industry to merge label and management functions.

A REUNION IN NASHVILLE

From where I sat in Waco as head of Word Records, we simply had to find a way to work with Mike and Dan on Reunion Records. Our success with Amy Grant on the Myrrh label was growing daily, and we knew that Mike understood talent and how to make great records. The decision was really very easy: We signed a distribution and marketing deal with Reunion Records.

In July of 1982, the Christian Booksellers Convention was held in Dallas, Texas, at the new downtown Hyatt Regency next to the brand-new Reunion Tower. Mike and Dan decided to launch Reunion Records and their first release, "Stubborn Love," from Kathy Troccoli at that event. Myrrh's marketing director at the time, Jeff Moseley, worked to make it all happen.

The event was a huge success. Reunion Records was like a racehorse breaking out of the gate. KT, as she became known, turned out to be a very successful artist, but the real reason

I did the deal with Reunion Records didn't emerge until the following year. His name was Michael W. Smith.

Smitty, as his friends know him, had come to Nashville in 1978. He worked for a landscaper as he pursued his songwriting and artist dreams. By 1981, he had become part of Meadowgreen Music, and his demo tape ended up on Mike Blanton's desk. That tape included "The Race Is On" and "You Need A Savior." Blanton told him, "You bring me 10 more songs like these two, and we'll do a record with you on our new label." Smitty came through. One of those next 10 songs was called "Friends!" Blanton was sold, and Smitty soon signed with Reunion and with Blanton Harrell Management.

I heard those demos too and wanted to sign Smitty to our Myrrh label at Word. That's when I found out that he was already committed to Mike and Dan. So the only way I could get him was by doing a marketing and distribution deal with them for Reunion.

As it turned out, Reunion was the perfect home for Smitty's music. Mike and Dan had grown up in the Church of Christ, so they really didn't have a church music background. They grew up listening to pop music. Their vision for the artists they served through Blanton Harrell Management and Reunion Records was really quite simple: "To make music (recorded and live music) that kids will be proud of and put it in the coolest venues." As it turned out, they did that very, very well for the next two decades.

REUNION RECORDS

Reunion was the perfect home for Michael W. Smith.

Of course, that vision didn't always line up well with the church

MORE ABOUT...JEFF MOSELEY

JEFF MOSELEY CAME TO WORD as a 20-year-old Baylor student from his job selling radio time for KRZI radio in Waco. A big part of Jeff's first job at Word was keeping Amy Grant songs played on the radio. He soon began directing the marketing plans for artists like Russ Taff, Mylon and Broken Heart, David Meece, Carman and Amy as General Manager of the Myrrh label.

Jeff left Word to join Mike Blanton and Dan Harrell at Reunion Records in 1986, and in 1989 he became the head of marketing and sales for us at Star Song. After helping build Star Song for the next eight years, he became the President of Benson and ultimately the owner of his own very successful labels, INO Records and Fair Trade Services. Jeff has delivered number one songs and best-selling artists at every stop along the way including Mercy Me's "I Can Only Imagine," Laura Story's "Blessings," and PC&D's "Revelation Song" in recent years.

In the process, Jeff has become a trusted friend who has guided me and many others through difficult times and hard decisions. My greatest joy has been watching young men I got to manage like Jeff, Roland Lundy, and many others build careers that have impacted so many lives.

establishment that was learning to accept early CCM artists. Shortly after Amy's ***Father's Eyes*** album hit the top of the charts, Mike (who was still working for Word at the time) and Dan decided that DeGarmo and Key would be a great choice for her band on the road.

As you can imagine, pairing sweet young Amy with a "long-haired" rock band didn't sit well with youth pastors who took the risk to bring Amy to do concerts in their churches. The backlash was often very strong. It didn't take Dan and Mike long to decide that Amy's concerts needed to be sponsored by those youth pastors, but actually take place at the local high school auditorium or art center.

Dan and Mike even once got a call from a well-known teacher who at the time was filling stadiums, who said, "I want you to know that I'm about to meet with 300 pastors and tell them that what Amy is doing is not of God."

It's hard to imagine, but youth pastors and that teacher weren't the only ones having a hard time with "sweet young Amy" becoming Amy with a band that rocked the house. At the 1981 Christian Artists Seminar in Estes Park, Colorado (an industry wide gathering of artists, labels, and fans), the audience response to Amy plus D&K was downright cold. No applause after the first three songs. But her plan was clear; Amy was determined to make music that would reach her generation…and we would all soon get on board.

That night, Mike and Dan became determined to make the best record in the history of Contemporary Christian Music. An album that "left NO ONE wondering if Amy loved the Lord or not." The next day they drove to Caribou Recording Studios just across the mountain from Estes Park and convinced the studio's owner, Jimmy Guercio, that Amy's

Michael W. Smith
© CCMMagazine.com

next album, ***Age to Age***, needed to be recorded there.

Dan and Mike also decided to utilize Amy's growing concert platform to introduce Michael W. Smith to CCM fans. He began by playing in Amy's band, but once he had his first record on the market, ***The Michael W. Smith Project***, he became Amy's opening act. Of course, Michael quickly became a huge concert draw all by himself.

Reunion Records continued to grow with artists like Pam Mark Hall, comedy group Ariel and Rich Mullins joining Kathy Troccoli on the label. It was clearly time to beef up the Reunion Records management team and the obvious answer was Jeff Moseley.

Jeff had managed all the marketing efforts for Amy and the Reunion artists for us at Word as the General Manager of Myrrh Records beginning in 1983. In 1986 he moved to Nashville and joined Mike and Dan at Reunion Records. His effect on both companies was enormous.

Chapter 15

TAKING CARE OF BUSINESS

Year after year, the key A&R leaders at Word, Sparrow, Benson and the growing list of smaller CCM-driven labels captured the creative expression of what God was doing in the lives of many singers, songwriters and producers. As Bill Gaither often said, "It's all about the song!" But those great artists, songwriters and producers also had to function in the real-life, real-time business world.

Record labels know how to finance, produce, market and distribute great music. But it really wasn't our job to pick the right concert promoter, keep the artist's bankbook in balance or make decisions about their personal lives.

That's why those artists needed managers and booking agents. Great managers like Dan Harrell and Mike Blanton were and are essential to helping Amy Grant, Michael W. Smith and other artists achieve the impact that has marked their careers. And booking agents like Charles Dorris, Jeff Roberts and John Huie were equally essential to delivering Contemporary Christian Music to large and small venues around the world.

Norman Miller was another one of those who managed many artist careers from obscurity to fame and fortune. I first met Norman in London in 1976 when he was on our Word UK staff. Over the next few years, Norman became a passionate and professional representative of many well-known artists including Sheila Walsh, Michael English, Twila Paris and Casting Crowns. His passion for the artist and the message they delivered was outstanding, and his passing in 2012 was a loss for us all.

Wes Yoder, the owner of The Ambassador Speakers Bureau, was my first contact with a manager. When we met in 1972, he was a young kid from Lancaster County, Pennsylvania. He drove one of those humongous 1970 Lincoln Continentals down Music Row in Nashville trying to tell the world about Randy Matthews (among others, I'm sure).

Wayne Coombs, who represented Andrae Crouch and Pat Boone for much of their CCM careers, set a high standard for all managers. The Wayne Coombs Agency also gave birth to the career of Dan Raines. Dan was so determined to learn from Wayne Coombs that he literally chased him down at a convention and made an offer Wayne could not refuse, "I won't even charge you— just hire me!"

Wayne did hire Dan, and his career was launched. It didn't take long for Pat Boone to realize that he needed Dan to run his Lamb & Lion record label. That decision gave Dan insight into the record label world while working with artists like Debby Boone, Dogwood and ultimately DeGarmo & Key.

I liked Dan so much that when Lamb & Lion was sold to Bob MacKenzie's Paragon/NewPax label, I hired him. He ultimately became the head of our Word Nashville office before forming his management company, Creative Trust.

Over the next two decades, Dan managed the careers of artists like Steven Curtis Chapman, Michael Card and Third Day. His plan to chase down Wayne Coombs sure paid off.

As Contemporary Christian Music grew in popularity, more and more managers appeared on the scene and Mike Atkins is certainly at the head of that list. It's hard to imagine the careers of Sandi Patty, Petra, 4Him, Wayne Watson, Jaci Velazquez, Point of Grace and Nicole C. Mullen without Mike's leadership.

SETTING THE RECORD EXECUTIVE STRAIGHT

In 1980, I met an artist manager named Zack Glickman. His clients included The Mighty Clouds of Joy, Dion and before long Russ Taff. I met Zack through signing a contract with the Clouds, and before long it was time to talk about doing Christian music with Dion (of Dion and the Belmonts).

When Zack flew to Waco for our meeting I was late picking him up. As he stood in the middle of the terminal, the American Airlines counter agent stepped out and asked him if he needed help. Zack told him he was waiting for a guy named Stan. The agent walked to the front door of the building, looked across the parking lot and said, "I don't see his car. He must be running late." I guess you could call that a home field advantage.

As we sat down to lunch at Ridgewood Country Club, I began with what I thought was a simple statement. "Zack, I know you know a lot about managing artists, but let me start by telling you about the Christian music business." He stopped me. "Oh, I already know all about the Christian music business."

Taken aback, I blurted out, "You do? Well then, why don't

you tell me." Zack explained, simply and confidently,

"THE CHRISTIAN MUSIC BUSINESS: SOMETIMES CHRISTIAN, SOMETIMES MUSIC, AND SOMETIMES BUSINESS."

I was stunned. This Jewish businessman had so succinctly described our business. Sometimes you can only get an accurate view through the eyes of an outsider, and sometimes truth can be very painful.

So let me take a moment and address any current or former Christian recording artist here. I'm sorry that we didn't do better with the delicate balance of music, business and Christian faith over the years. I'm sorry that we told you that we believed in you and your music, but failed to tell you that we'd have to move on to another artist if your music didn't work commercially.

DID YOU KNOW?

Dion DiMucci (Dion and the Belmonts) first reached the top of the pop charts as a teenager in 1958 with "I Wonder Why." A string of hit songs including "A Teenager In Love," and "Abraham Martin and John" helped make Dion a household name. He was born again in late 1979, and subsequently released five CCM albums for DaySpring Records, winning a Dove Award in 1984 for the album *I Put Away My Idols.*

For many, you depended far too much on your contract

with a record label to validate your music and ministry. And sometimes we ignored the pain we caused you through what must have been perceived as rejection of you as a person and your art or your message. Far too often we just moved on without any explanation, and I am truly sorry.

A MANAGER, A LAWYER AND A ROOM FULL OF REPORTERS

We needed managers and we needed booking agents, and of course, we needed lawyers. Obviously, an artist like Amy Grant needed the best of all three.

Amy's sales momentum grew with the release of her third Myrrh album, ***Never Alone***. But with the release of that album she had fulfilled her recording agreement with Word. So the big contract negotiation was on. That meant many intense discussions with her manager, Dan Harrell, and a flood of documents from their attorney, Randy Smith.

Dan insisted that we agree to a guaranteed number of units to be sold on each Amy record under the new agreement. I'd never done a contract with that type of financial risk, but I reluctantly agreed to guarantee royalty payments to Amy for 200,000 units of the combined sales of three albums. That guarantee was a stretch since ***Never Alone*** had sold around 100,000 units.

When it seemed that the new deal was done, we decided to make the new Amy Grant – Myrrh agreement the focal point of our National Press Days event in Waco. We knew the contract was big news in our industry.

The day of the press event began at 8 AM with Randy Smith, Dan and me in the offices of our Word attorney, Danny Pleitz. We talked through some very minor language adjustments to the contract and then Dan Harrell and I left Danny and Randy to work out the details.

Twelve hours later they were still working on those details! Their meeting eventually moved to Waco's Fish Pond Country Club where we were meeting with the press. That evening as I sat on the piano bench next to Amy announcing this brand-new contract, I saw Dan Harrell urgently waving at me from the back of the room. Clearly something was wrong. I smiled and asked Amy to play a new song for our audience as I slipped to the back of the room. Dan said, "They are in an office back there, and there's about to be a fight! We'd better do something and quick."

We opened the office door to an astonishing scene. Danny Pleitz was standing on one side of the desk, shaking

▼ Amy Grant
© CCMMagazine.com

his fist (which was in a cast) at Randy Smith. No, there wasn't going to be a fight. They were just doing their jobs. We saw two fine lawyers advocating for their clients, but after 12 hours of non-stop negotiation over "words in a document," they both needed some relief. In five minutes Dan Harrell and I agreed on the language that was causing the ruckus, and we all shook hands. Well, Danny Pleitz did the best he could with the cast.

Yes, *sometimes* it's Christian, *sometimes* music and *sometimes* very intense business. Sometimes we kept the three in balance. And sometimes we didn't.

Chapter 16

THE GREAT DIVIDE

Re-signing Amy Grant in 1981 was a milestone for us at Myrrh Records. We were good to go for another three albums. It didn't take long to discover, however, that the Christian music industry was a far cry from "good to go." In just a few short weeks we began to realize that 1981 was going to be a very difficult year. We all needed some good news.

Evie's sales disappeared almost as fast as she had from that stage in Minneapolis just one year earlier. Then Russ Taff left the Imperials to pursue a solo career. And Amy had been without a new studio album for almost two years.

On top of that, Jarrell McCracken agreed to sell Ralph Carmichael our 50% of Light Records, and Ralph launched his own sales force. The steady stream of Praise Albums and Kids Praise Product from Maranatha!Music, along with sales from our Southern gospel Canaan label and our new Black gospel label, Rejoice, helped us avoid a layoff.

Things were not much better at Benson and Sparrow. Just a year earlier, Keith Green asked Billy Ray to release him from the remaining two records on his Sparrow contract. Keith said the Lord told him to give his records away.

Billy Ray faced a monumental decision. He had formed

Sparrow with a clear mission: "To make it possible for artists to do the ministry God had called them to do." Letting Keith go would be painful but making him stay would violate the very principle upon which Sparrow was founded. In the end, Billy Ray released him.

However, there was some very good news on the horizon for Sparrow. Greg Nelson's success as Sandi Patty's producer had opened the doorway to a great personal friendship with Bill Gaither. At the time, Bill's band included a group of young musicians: Billy Smiley played trumpet, Mark Gershmel, trombone and keys, Gary Lunn played bass, and a world- class guitar player named Dann Huff.

After sound check and rehearsals were finished, they would begin to work on their own compositions. When the guys decided to record five demos, Steve Green, a backup singer for the Gaither Trio, offered to sing them. Chris Christian, who had formed Home Sweet Home Records a couple of years earlier at the urging of Bob MacKenzie, signed Whiteheart to Home Sweet Home Records and released their self-titled album, "Whiteheart," after all the other major labels had passed on signing the group. It would soon hit the top of the CCM charts.

While Whiteheart was just getting off the ground, Steve Green was also a member of the Gaither Vocal Band and touring full time with the Gaithers. Within a year of Whiteheart's release Steve left the group. While he loved the music, he would later admit that he was wandering without real direction and felt restless.

At that point, Greg Nelson and Steve met at the Paragon publishing office to discuss his recording future. Greg knew exactly what to do. Since the day Billy Ray had forgiven Greg the $76,000 debt he incurred with Spirit records, Greg had waited for this moment. Greg contacted Billy Ray about Steve Green joining the Sparrow roster. Billy Ray invited Steve to spend a few days in California to see if they really were called to work together. It was soon clear to both men that Steve Green belonged on the Sparrow label.

During the months between the time Steve signed with Sparrow and began to record, he went through a profound spiritual awakening. At a family gathering, Steve's older brother, Randy, confronted Steve about his nominal Christianity and need for revival. That confrontation led to a gracious work of God and a radical change. Steve had a new purpose and direction.

Billy Ray had been banking on the fact that Steve still toured with the Gaithers and would benefit from that platform. But with the new change came an urgency to do something very specific. When Steve left the Gaithers, Billy Ray had to make a hard decision—keep Steve with no platform or release him from the contract. Billy Ray chose to stay the course.

With the release of his first album, aptly titled Steve Green, Steve became a major artist for Sparrow and our industry.

The story in Nashville at the Benson Company was much like our story at Word. Benson had been built on the success of many great Southern gospel artists like The Speers, The Rambos and The Downings. The Bill Gaither Trio and Doug Oldham were also huge sellers in the more traditional church music world.

Bob MacKenzie and his boss, Bob Benson Jr., certainly didn't ignore the growing Contemporary Christian Music market. They had launched the Greentree label in 1976 to house their growing roster that included major artists like Reba Rambo, Dallas Holm, Tim Shepherd, Andrus Blackwood and Company, Phil Johnson, Glad, and Harvest. By the late 70's, Benson was distributing Petra and DeGarmo and Key records as well.

But something had clearly changed for all of us by 1981. After watching sales decline for most of that year, I called our executive team together and delivered a challenge: "For the last few years we have lived off the momentum created by the Jesus Movement. It has taken a decade for that tidal wave to sweep across the U.S. and now that wave has ended. We're about to find out if we have a real business here or not."

FROM AGE TO AGE

As I drove from Waco to Dallas on Saturday, January 9, 1982, I really wasn't sure we could sustain the company at the expense level we had built. We had held our December sales conference three weeks earlier and I didn't see any momentum-changing album releases on the horizon. I was very concerned.

As I drove north on Interstate 35, I decided to play a tape that Mike Blanton, Amy Grant's manager, had sent me earlier that week. In those days, labels sometimes just gave the production money to the artist and his or her team. They selected the songs, hired the producer and made the record. So this was my first time to hear the new Amy Grant project. It had been more than two years since we had heard any new music from her and I really needed to hear something good.

What I heard was not good. It was spectacular. After almost 10 years as the head of sales and marketing, I knew a hit song when I heard one and that tape had at least *five* hit songs.

The next day at Tom Stipe's house in Denver, I watched my Dallas Cowboys lose to the San Francisco 49ers in the NFL Championship Game at Candlestick Park. Do you remember where you were when Everson Walls let Dwight Clark get behind him in the end zone?

I wasn't happy about that game but I knew it was "game on" for our company. We had been handed the album that just might turn the entire industry around.

I quickly called Dan Johnson who headed up marketing

and product development for all our Word labels at the time, and set the plan in action. We would rent one of the restored mansions in downtown Waco and invite our record and music staff to have lunch and listen to this new Amy Grant album. Dan Harrell and Mike Blanton would join us.

As we sat and listened, I watched the faces of key members of our team—folks like Dan Hickling, Allen Weed, Vonnie Jandrain, Brenda Boswell and Lynn Nichols. They had lived through a very difficult 1981 and they probably wondered why we were spending money renting a mansion and throwing a lunch party for them. But song after song won them over.

"In A Little While," "Sing Your Praise," "I Have Decided," and finally "El Shaddai." Everyone in the room knew—it really was *Game On*. As the final notes subsided, I spoke to the group. "What you have just heard will turn our company around. From this day forward, I don't care what you were doing. I want you to spend 90% of your time making this album a success." I meant exactly that and they all agreed.

Age to Age hit the market in May 1982. By Christmas we had sold over 200,000 copies and that number climbed daily. It eventually sold more than 3 million copies.

The year that had started with such uncertainly ended with a bang; that one album seemed to turn the entire market around. Customers came back to the stores to buy ***Age to Age***, and while they were there, they bought a lot of other albums as well. It also helped that the cassette was finally emerging as a viable form for music.

In 1982, Sparrow took a giant step forward too. Sheila Walsh and Michelle Pillar entered the scene, and the Talbots continued to sell records, along with Second Chapter and Scott Wesley Brown. Early 1983 also brought us Steve Taylor's "I Want To Be A Clone," and he became one of the very first artists to use visual media to generate thousands of young fans.

In Nashville, the Benson Company had their own ***Age to Age*** story in the works on the Bill Gaither Trio stage. Everything was set for the Sandi Patty explosion that would change our industry as well.

▲ Dan Johnson, Roland Lundy and Amy Grant celebrate the success of Age to Age. © Word Music Entertainment

ON THE ROAD AGAIN

Mike Blanton and Dan Harrell were the best management team in the industry at the time and they had the track record to prove it. They didn't just react to Amy's success; they were very proactive in placing her on just the right television, publicity and concert platforms. And the plan worked.

They capitalized on the sales success of ***Age to Age*** throughout 1982 and '83 as Amy drew thousands of fans to every event on her calendar. The culmination of the ***Age to Age*** tour for me occurred in December 1983 at the Universal Amphitheatre in Los Angeles, California. No other Christian artist had dared to book a concert in that massive 6200-seat auditorium, but that didn't deter Mike and Dan.

Amy sold out that venue two nights in a row. Success at the Amphitheatre was of course just another step along the pathway of Amy's astounding career trajectory. Over the next few months, Mike and Dan's strategy led to television appearances, a concert at Radio City Music Hall, opening for Kenny Rogers on the road and constant exposure in magazines and newspapers across the country.

Age to Age sold so well that we decided to record a Christmas album for release in the fall of 1983 rather than a new studio record. We didn't want to do anything to slow down the radio and retail momentum of ***Age to Age***, and a Christmas album would come and go from the marketplace very quickly and set up her next studio record to be released in 1984.

In the summer of 1983, Amy, Gary Chapman (Amy's husband and highly successful songwriter), Mike, Dan and Brown Bannister went back to Caribou Studios (where ***Age to Age*** had been recorded) just above Boulder, Colorado, to record the Christmas album. What we thought would be a good-selling album and nice transition from ***Age to Age*** to the next studio record turned into another momentum surge for Amy.

"Tennessee Christmas" took all the last-minute creativity that Amy and Gary could muster. Gary had completed the melody of the song, but when it came time to record, the lyrics just weren't right. Brown had already recorded the music tracks and it was time to finish, but without lyrics, that's pretty hard to do. While Amy sang the part of the lyrics that was finished to the pre-recorded tracks, Gary was upstairs writing the next verse. Once he got the lyric he wanted on paper, he would race downstairs, re-work it with Amy, and then she would record the verse.

After so many years in the industry I was still astounded

at how hit songs would come together, and "Tennessee Christmas" was definitely a hit. Radio stations – Christian, pop and country – all gave it a lot of airtime.

While Mike Blanton and Dan Harrell opened door after door into key concerts, television and publicity opportunities for Amy, our team at Word was working hard to place her products on the shelves of every mainstream record outlet in the country. From Tower Records to K-Mart, Walmart, Target and beyond, we were finally able to convince retailers that Contemporary Christian Music buyers were in their stores and ready to spend some cash.

> **DID YOU KNOW?**
>
> ***Straight Ahead*** **was the first Christian album to chart on the Billboard pop album chart. The song "Angels" was a number one Christian radio hit for 13 weeks. In addition, Amy won a Grammy for "Best Gospel Performance, Female." The album was certified gold in 1985.**

Then we began working on Amy's next album. We had many discussions with Mike and Dan about the title and cover. When we boiled it all down, it made sense that the next album would be called ***Straight Ahead***. Those two words summed up our collective strategy for Amy.

Chapter 17

MORE THAN WONDERFUL

Amy Grant wasn't the only artist who packed out major venue after venue. Sandi Patty was experiencing the same upsurge in her own touring schedule, and Mike Atkins had a great deal to do with that.

Mike Atkins came into the Contemporary Christian Music industry in 1984, right in the midst of a very successful career as a boxing manager and promoter. I'm sure boxing prepared him well for our industry!

Mike was in Nashville promoting an ESPN fight night, but he was also in town to see his future wife, Debbie, who worked for the Benson Company. And that is how he came face to face with Benson's CFO, Tom Bates, and their President, Wayne Erickson.

The executive team at Benson wanted to upgrade Sandi's touring opportunities, so Tom and Wayne asked Mike to promote "just one Sandi show" in Fort Wayne, Indiana. It would be Sandi's first concert outside a church venue and they knew it had to be handled right. Maybe that's why they reached outside the CCM world for a promoter. Because that concert was such a huge success, Mike became an integral part of Sandi's arena tour dates for several years.

DON'T GO PAST 11

After Sandi left Benson and signed with Word, one of Mike Atkins' tour dates included New York City's Radio City Music Hall. It quickly became a sellout. That allowed the marketing guys at Word Records to unleash a massive promotion plan for Sandi's new record on subway placards and bus benches across the area.

Mike was thrilled with the sellout crowd but very concerned about the cost of doing a show in New York City. So Mike made it clear to Sandi, "Whatever you do, don't go past 11 PM. The show costs go through the roof if we are even one minute over time."

As the evening began, the audience seemed to enjoy the show but they were somewhat reserved. Sandi had done the

IN CONCERT. SANDI PATTY WITH FIRST CALL.
Sandi, Bonnie Keen, Marty McCall, and Melodie Tunney.
Courtesy of Melodie Tunney

current show so many times that she knew where the audience response typically came but it was not happening that night. So Sandi decided to add a medley to alter the end of the show as Mike watched the clock.

Finally the crowd came to life. People began cheering and even bringing flowers to the stage. When she finished the last note she walked off the stage right past Mike. With a sly grin she winked and tapped her watch. One minute before 11!

As you can imagine many funny moments emerged from the major concerts Mike promoted each year. At one of his many Petra tour dates at the Westbury Music Fair, the plan called for the band to emerge from a stage that ascended in the middle of the auditorium.

As the stage rose to the proper level, Louie Weaver, the band's drummer, lifted his drumsticks in the air and ran around the stage, but he didn't see the stairwell at the back of the stage. I'm sure that the audience wondered why Louie just vanished!

Such is life on the road. Sometimes funny. Sometimes awe-inspiring. And sometimes just another show. But the message of hope that only Jesus can bring was always front and center.

WE SHALL BEHOLD HIM

Over the years, I often saw major artists like Andrae Crouch or Evie create space in the market with their music and personality. When that artist vacated that space the market demanded another artist to fill that void.

Andrae Crouch made room for Leon Patillo who would make room for BeBe and CeCe Winans. The Imperials would one day make room for 4 Him. Evie made room for the very church-friendly Amy Grant. And as Amy expanded beyond the normal "church market" she created space for Sandi Patty.

Sandi was not an overnight success but she was a phenomenon. She began as a young girl singing with her father in the Ron Patty Trio and then attended Anderson University in Anderson, Indiana.

Her career began with a "custom album" called ***For My Friends*** produced by Randy Hammel. A custom album is a product that artists sell in concerts rather than through stores. It pays some bills for artists who do not have a recording contract.

Randy asked another Anderson University student named Neal Joseph to help with arrangements and background vocals. Neal had been trained through three years of work with The Sound Generation while he attended John Brown University. He had also spent time on the road as part of a very significant group called Truth.

Soon, ***For My Friends*** ended up on the desk of Phil Brower who headed up Zondervan's contemporary record label, Milk & Honey Records. Phil knew talent when he heard it and he signed Sandi to his label.

Phil also made another good decision when he combined Sandi's great talent with Neal Joseph's arranging and producing skills. ***Sandi's Song*** was the result. That album featured one of the great songs in Christian music history, "The Day He Wore My Crown," written by Phil Johnson.

Milk & Honey Records didn't work out for Zondervan, and they soon lost their key artists to other labels. Wayne Watson came to Word's DaySpring label. Michael Card went to Sparrow. Harvest went to Benson. Twila Paris to Star Song. And after just one Sandi record with Milk and Honey, Neal

Neal and the orchestra knew Sandi was destined for Contemporary Christian Music greatness. And it wasn't long before the entire CCM world knew.

Sandi was already touring with The Bill Gaither Trio as a background singer and Bill made sure that a vast audience and market heard this special young lady sing night after night. During the second half of each show, Sandi moved to the middle of the stage and delivered "We Shall Behold Him" with her astounding vocal performance. And the newest CCM star was just beginning to soar.

When Neal Joseph left the Benson Company in late 1981 to work for Word, his days as Sandi's producer came to an end, but Sandi Patty was just getting started. She would soon join forces with Greg Nelson and impact millions of lives.

THERE IS A REDEEMER

1982 turned out to be a year of great breakthrough for our industry but it also brought great tragedy. On July 28, Keith Green and 11 others were killed in a plane crash that occurred on the property of Last Days Ministries in Lindale, Texas.

I never knew Keith Green personally. As his connection with Sparrow was birthed and grew, I was busy in my own little world--too busy to make the effort to know him.

▲ Keith & Melody Green
© CCMMagazine.com

That was my loss.

I have heard many stories of his great kindness to the disadvantaged and his prophet-like stance regarding the things of God. I didn't know Keith but I do know his songs and his legacy. I believe the lyrics to one of his most famous songs, "There Is A Redeemer," clearly reveals the reason I'm writing this book.

I'm so grateful that there really is a Redeemer—Jesus, God's own Son. He's still in the redemption business today. If He can do something good with my life, He can do the same for you.

Chapter 18

GOD GAVE ROCK 'N' ROLL TO YOU

The industry sales crisis had come to an end and that made us all very busy. The fans came back to the stores and bought thousands of albums from a burgeoning new wave of contemporary Christian artists. *Age to Age* became the rising tide that floats all boats with Sandi Patty and Michael W. Smith waiting in the wings. Contemporary Christian Music was indeed alive and well and rocking the house...literally.

FROM THE GAME ROOM TO THE TURNTABLE

Darrell Harris and Wayne Donowho, the owners of Star Song headquartered in Houston, seemed to understand Christian rock and roll better than other label execs. Back in 1977, they had noticed the upsurge of teenagers playing video games in the malls around Houston and they also noticed the music that blared in every game room.

STAR SONG

In 1977, Darrell Harris & Wayne Donowho, the owners of Star Song headquartered in Houston, seemed to understand Christian rock and roll better than other label execs.

They relentlessly asked Christian radio stations, artists and anyone else they knew, "Where is the Christian band that makes music in that language?" The answer always seemed to be, "They don't exist." And to the mainstream Christian radio station that was correct.

However, Darrell and Wayne were not easily discouraged. They kept asking.-One day they stopped by United Saints Christian music store in Pasadena, Texas, and asked the owner, Jimmy Wommack, if he had heard any music that could reach those kids in the game rooms. "Yep," he answered, "Resurrection Band."

Darrell and Wayne had never heard of them. So Jimmy asked if they knew about Jesus People USA. They didn't, so Jimmy educated them. The next day Darrell called Jesus People USA and got Glenn Kaiser on the phone. Glenn and his wife, Wendi, led Resurrection Band.

DID YOU KNOW?

Rez Band's album, *Awaiting Your Reply*, was recorded for $8,000 over a two-week period of all-night recording sessions.

When Darrell asked if they had a record label deal, Glenn didn't sound very interested. "We made our own record ***Awaiting Your Reply*** and sent it to Word, Maranatha, Benson and Sparrow. Everybody rejected it. I don't think you'll like it either." But Darrell convinced Glenn to send a copy.

As soon as Darrell began to play that album in the studio control room he wept. It was an answer to prayer. It didn't take him long to enter a distribution deal with Jesus People USA and distribute their first two records, ***Awaiting Your Reply*** and

Rainbow's End. They were the first two Christian rock records to sell more than 100,000 units. In 2008, *Christianity Today* called Resurrection Band "the most influential band in Christian music history."

When Dan Brock, manager of Petra, saw what Star Song had done with Rez Band, he knew Star Song was right for Petra. He sent Darrell a demo tape of Petra's recording of "Why Should the Father Bother." Darrell was hooked, and Star Song ultimately created and delivered 10 Petra Records to devoted fans around the world.

By 1981, in spite of its success with Rez Band and Petra, Star Song was in serious need of cash to keep the company alive. That prompted a call to me at Word from Wayne Donowho.

▼ EARLY PETRA, Bob Hartman, John DeGroff, Bill Glover, Greg Hough
© CCMMagazine.com

MORE ABOUT... TWILA PARIS

It's hard to imagine that the same producer who brought us Petra's "Judas Kiss" also brought us Twila Paris' "The Warrior Is A Child." But Jonathan David Brown did. Twila's next album, *Kingdom Seekers*, was released through Star Song in 1982. It included her powerful song "He Is Exalted."

As the last days of the studio production on *Kingdom Seekers* approached, Jonathan, Twila and Darrell Harris realized they needed one more great song for the album. They solicited songs from every publisher Darrell knew, but nothing right emerged. Finally Darrell asked Twila if she had anything – maybe something unfinished or that was perhaps just lying in her piano bench at home.

Suddenly, Jonathan remembered a song that they considered but did not use for the album. Twila said, *"I don't know how good it is, but I'll sing it for you." And she sang "Lamb of God!"*

That phone call quickly turned into a trip to Waco for Wayne and Darrell. They definitely needed cash, and a lot of it, to sustain the Star Song label. They still had one year left on their distribution deal with Bob MacKenzie and Wayne Erickson at the Benson Company. However, Benson was having a cash struggle as well. The bottom line was that if Word could advance $200,000 to Star Song, they could get out of their Benson deal and we could distribute them.

During that meeting, Darrell played a cassette recording of three new Petra songs. I tried not to show my enthusiasm, but let's be real—the first song was "More Power To Ya." There was no doubt in my mind; we were going to make this deal happen. And we did.

In hindsight, advancing $200,000 to Star Song was a good move, but at the time it was an enormous risk. I needed some kind of insurance, so we literally took possession of all the Petra masters and their signed artist contract. We placed all of it in a safe deposit box at Citizen's National Bank in Waco. If Wayne and Darrell didn't come through with a new Petra record, we would.

Of course, Petra soared and began to fill auditoriums. The strength of Word's distribution system helped us sell five times what Benson had sold on Petra. Star Song was quickly able to repay the full advance and brought us a steady flow of hit albums from Petra, Twila Paris, Steve and Annie Chapman, Farrell and Farrell and many others.

A BAND CALLED MEMPHIS

FROM LEFT: Eddie DeGarmo, Dana Key, Greg Morrow (drums), Tommy Cathey (bass)
© CCMMagazine.com

Eddie DeGarmo and Dana Key grew up in Memphis, Tennessee, and they became friends in the first grade. They formed their first band in the sixth grade and recorded their first album for High Records (a label started by Al Green) when they were 15.

They were typical teenage musicians of that 70's era until God suddenly interrupted their rock-and-roll lifestyle. For some reason, Eddie decided to attend a Dave Wilkerson crusade meeting in Memphis in 1974. When Eddie went forward to receive Jesus as Lord and Savior, his prayer counselor just happened to be Dallas Holm. Eddie's life was simply changed. Forever. He knew he had to introduce Dana to this Jesus. They both skipped school the next day and Eddie led Dana to the Lord.

They didn't know what to do with their newfound faith except to write songs that expressed what was going on in their hearts. There was no career path in Christian music, much less

Christian rock. So they just wrote and performed songs about Jesus wherever they could.

Eddie and Dana heard Resurrection Band play at a local park and soon they became friends with the Rez Band's Glenn and Wendi Kaiser. That couple had reached hundreds of musicians over the early years of Contemporary Christian Music, and DeGarmo and Key would never be the same.

In the following year, Eddie and Dana heard their first Petra record. They were hooked; they knew they had to use the new songs they were writing to tell everybody they could about Jesus. Of course, not everyone wanted to hear Christian rock music. They were actually kicked off of college campuses and even had tomatoes thrown at them in one concert.

As students at Memphis State University, they both went to work for Campus Life Ministries, a part of Youth For Christ founded by Bill Bright. One day, Campus Life sent their writer, Steve Lawhead, to Memphis to write an article for their magazine.

Steve, who was also the music reviewer for the magazine, asked to hear the music demo that DeGarmo and Key had recorded.

He left town with a cassette of the demo and Eddie never gave it another thought until he got a letter from Billy Ray Hearn at Sparrow Records. Evidently, Lawhead had told Billy Ray about this new rock band in Memphis.

Then, out of the blue, the phone rang at Eddie's apartment. "Is this Eddie DeGarmo?"

"Yes, it is."

Eddie, this is Pat Boone. I heard your music and I want to talk to you about recording for my label Lamb & Lion Records."

Pat Boone was a huge celebrity in those days so Eddie

assumed it was a prank call by one of his friends; he hung up.

Pat called right back, "Eddie, this really is Pat Boone. Please don't hang up." The next week, Pat flew to Memphis with his son-in-law, Doug Corbin, who ran Lamb & Lion. They struck a deal to record DeGarmo & Key.

Word distributed the first two D&K albums on Lamb & Lion. Then the label moved to the Benson Company for distribution. Pat and his partner, Mike Curb, were already unhappy with the way Benson handled Lamb and Lion's recent Debby Boone release. When DeGarmo and Key's first albums didn't sell very well either, Pat and Mike wanted to terminate Lamb and Lion's distribution through Benson.

Bob MacKenzie at Benson just knew DeGarmo and Key would be a success. So he agreed to release Lamb & Lion from their contract in exchange for "this little rock band from Memphis." In 1983, DeGarmo and Key released ***Mission of Mercy*** on Benson's Power Discs label. D&K had their first hit album.

DID YOU KNOW?

Pat Boone wanted to change the name of the group to Memphis but Eddie and Dana just couldn't do that. Looking back, Eddie agreed. "Calling the group Memphis was a great idea actually. That was the era of super groups like Boston and Chicago. There is no telling how much impact we could have had on pop radio if we could have seen that possibility."

NO TURNING BACK

In 2010, long after they had finished their touring days, Eddie and Dana were invited to perform at a Christian biker rally at the LifeWay Retreat Center in Ridgecrest, North Carolina.

After the event, Eddie and his son-in-law drove back to Nashville. Dana stayed behind to take a flight back to Memphis the next morning. At 1:30 AM, as he rode silently toward Nashville, Eddie answered Dana's phone call. "Hey, I've been thinking. Wouldn't it be cool if we got in the Hall of Fame the same year as Cash! You know, a real Memphis connection." Eddie said, "Yeah, that would be cool. OK, be safe."

A couple of hours later that early morning, a pulmonary embolism blocked the blood flow to Dana's heart and brought his life on this earth to an end, and our industry lost another great musician and friend to so many. A few weeks later, Eddie DeGarmo and Dana Key *were* inducted into the Gospel Music Hall of Fame along with Johnny Cash.

Chapter 19
THIS MEANS WAR

Thanks to music pioneers like Petra, Rez Band and D&K, the acceptance of Christian rock was growing across the country. Even my old friend Ralph Carmichael released a rock band called Servant on his label. But he was just one of many who saw the opportunity to utilize Christian rock to reach the masses.

In California, Frontline Records became home to groups like Bloodgood, Daniel Amos, Idle Cure, Altar Boys and Wild Blue Yonder (featuring then 15-year-old Crystal Lewis). Benson distributed them. Jimmy Kempner, who owned Frontline knew how to recognize talent, and his head of sales, Kent Songer, proved he could sell a lot of records. In fact, I've been told that MC Hammer considered signing with Frontline as he began his music career.

Frontline releases were cutting edge and were often in conflict with established church leadership. The backlash from church leaders was strong and relentless. I didn't blame them. Sometimes it was difficult for me to accept radical rock music as a viable tool for communicating the gospel. But it was.

The Benson Company was more than happy to distribute

all these releases along with one of the biggest Christian rock groups of all time, Stryper. Can you imagine what a Benson sales conference was like in those days? "First we have a new song from Sandi Patty. Now let's listen to the newest release from Stryper. And then we'll get to the new Speer Family album."

WITHOUT HIM

Christian rock seemed full of very unusual characters. In 1981, Buck Herring of Second Chapter of Acts asked me to meet with one of the most unusual of them all – Mylon LeFevre.

I knew the basic outline of Mylon's story: He was born into The Singing LeFevres (a well-known Southern gospel group), wrote the gospel standard "Without Him" (which Elvis Presley and many others recorded), eventually became a drug addict and traveled the world as the opening act for Eric Clapton, George Harrison and a host of other rock stars. His life had been a well-chronicled mess and I had enough messes in my own life at the time.

What I didn't know was that in 1980, Mylon surrendered his life to Christ at a Second Chapter of Acts concert. He quit secular music, moved back to Atlanta and became a janitor at Mount Paran Church of God and began making Christian music. He had released his first Christian album on the MCA Songbird label a year earlier and had sold a whopping 9,000 copies.-

I really didn't have any time for him but Buck insisted. Mylon was due at my office at 10 AM but finally showed up two hours late. I wasn't happy about the two-hour delay and I was far too busy to waste much time on this guy.

As Mylon walked into my office, I quietly told my secretary, Claudine, to remind me of an important meeting in 10 minutes. Mylon was a perfect caricature of a rock musician. He stood about 6 foot 2 and weighed maybe 150 pounds. His long, jet-black hair hung over his shoulders. With his muttonchops he looked like Elvis. He wore a chartreuse jump suit with a six-inch cross dangling from his neck.

Mylon spoke very slowly with a Southern drawl and he insisted on showing me a scrapbook of pictures with him and about every drugged-out rock star of the 70's. I was not impressed, but just before my secretary came to interrupt our meeting the Lord spoke clearly to me, "You're going to be connected with this guy the rest of your life."

▼ Mylon Le Fevre
© CCMMagazine.com

IMPACTING THE NEXT GENERATION. Stryper
© CCMMagazine.com

I had learned to trust that "inner voice" more and more over the last few years. I told Claudine to cancel the other meeting and I began to listen to Mylon intently. That was the beginning of a long friendship.

I had the privilege of being involved with Mylon in the making of 10 records over the next decade or so. Yes, we sold a lot of records. But more importantly, I got to watch God use one of those "radical Christian rockers" lead thousands of lost young people into a life-changing encounter with Jesus Christ.

Meanwhile, the storms over Christian Rock raged on. Bill Gothard, Paul Crouch, Jimmy Swaggart, David Wilkerson and other Christian leaders condemned Christian Rock from pulpits and TV screens across the world. As I have told many musicians, "Music will always pass you by." And Christian rock music certainly passed a lot of well-known and well-meaning church leaders.

In my view, music is simply a tool, a conduit. Whether we call it traditional, contemporary, rock, gospel, or Southern gospel, Christian music can, has and will continue to carry the message of Jesus. And in spite of many efforts to discredit Christian rock groups, D&K, Rez Band, Petra, Mylon and Broken Heart, and Stryper did deliver the message of Jesus to a growing number of fans that desperately needed to hear the truth in a language they could understand. I'll always be grateful for the opportunity to help make that happen.

▲ From Top Left: Rich Mullins, Rebecca St. James, Michael English, Steven Curtis Chapman, Twila Paris, Carman, 4HIM (Andy Chrisman, Mark Harris, Marty Magehee & Kirk Sullivan)

GOTTA' SERVE SOMEBODY

1985 –1995

Chapter 20

TAKING IT TO THE STREETS

Amy Grant's next album, *Straight Ahead*, was successful but did not duplicate the sales success of *Age to Age*. We knew that putting albums on the shelves in mainstream stores required airplay on pop radio stations. We also knew that we were making a product that could compete with the music from secular labels like CBS Records, Polygram, RSO, Warner, Elektra and other music giants of the day.

It was time for a new strategy if we were going to break through that wall. We knew we needed a partnership with a major secular label. And we soon found ourselves at A&M Records (the whole story was told in Chapter 1).

Amy's new 1985 release, ***Unguarded,*** would soon become the first Contemporary Christian album to be marketed simultaneously on a Christian label (Myrrh) to Christian radio and retailers and on a pop label (A&M) to pop radio and general market retail stores. The final hurdle between our music and the masses was now gone.

Our agreement with A&M Records brought our music into mainstream radio and retail like never before. What we had reluctantly called Contemporary Christian Music just 10 years earlier had become a household term in the church and would soon become part of pop music history. All the struggles, all the meetings, all the sales pitches and contract negotiations had led us to that historic agreement.

Looking back on that moment, I now realize how appropriate it was to be in the same studio where the world's most celebrated musical artists birthed music that literally fed starving people across the ocean. We were on a mission as well—to take Christ to a world starving for hope.

With one deal, our industry was changed forever. Over the next 10 years, our CCM labels would deliver many pop hits through A&M's competitors as well. And every major Christian record label would be acquired by the largest secular music companies in the world. Along the way we would all realize, it's hard to be "in the world" and not be consumed by it.

The CCM industry had never been in such great shape. It seemed like every label was selling more and more product. The A&M deal opened doors that we had only dreamed about. But I was facing a new and very personal challenge.

▼ Brown Bannister, Peter York, and future Sparrow artist & renowned producer, Charlie Peacock.

At that point in my career, my whole adult life had been spent in the trenches--making the deals, convincing retailers to focus on our albums and touching many aspects of our product development and marketing strategies. For me, those were the best parts of the business. But as our executive team at Word expanded, my role shifted into more business planning and a lot more involvement with our owners at ABC, Inc.

Nothing in business invigorates me more than hearing a great song and creating marketing plans to take it into the lives of people who need it. Crunching numbers or sitting in a boring meeting to determine "who is going to park where in the parking lot" just does not do it for me. But that's where I often found myself.

Of course, change is a constant in business and in life. We all go through seasons of doing what we don't like or did not expect. About the same time that I was forced into a new role, Billy Ray Hearn also found himself in the grip of an unexpected and very painful change.

In 1984, Billy Ray's wife, Joan, died after a long bout with cancer. Although crushed by her passing, Billy Ray saw the need to change some things at Sparrow. He told me, "After Joan's death I realized how fragile life really is, and I wanted to implement a plan for the long-term future of Sparrow."

He didn't have to look far for the young men who would carry Sparrow into the future. He turned to his son, Bill, and son-in-law, Rick Horne. Bill was already a well-respected marketing and sales executive in our industry, and Rick ran the administration and finance department of Sparrow.

Billy Ray also invited a young man named Peter York to come to California to run their publishing department. Peter had been a successful member of Phil Keaggy's Love Inn Band for many years. When Peter joined the team, Billy Ray soon realized that he had a very talented product-development guy to join with Bill in marketing and Rick in administration.

With Bill and Peter making more of the product and marketing decisions, Sparrow's sales continued to grow. By 1985, the management team was in place and sales were increasing with Steve Green, Sheila Walsh, Steve Taylor and the other ministry-oriented artists at Sparrow like Michael Card, Steve Camp and John Michael Talbot. But like the rest of us, Sparrow had room for another major artist.

When Billy Ray had forgiven the $76,000 loan to Greg Nelson years earlier, he could not have dreamed how it would come back to him—and more than once. But it did.

A STAR IS BORN AT OPRYLAND

In 1986, Greg Nelson heard a bluegrass band playing on one of the side stages at the Opryland theme park in Nashville. One of the members was Steven Curtis Chapman. He played banjo and guitar and I hear he was a pretty good clogger as well!

Steven and his wife, Mary Beth, had moved to Nashville a year earlier from a small town in Kentucky. Like many others, he came to Nashville to pursue his musical dreams. Playing at Opryland wasn't exactly a destination job but with that and Steven's day job in the Benson warehouse, he and Mary Beth managed to stay afloat.

Greg Nelson had recently entered an agreement to find writers for a new publishing company called 19th Street Productions. He signed Steven Curtis Chapman as a songwriter and when they needed a record label for him, Greg once again honored his commitment to Billy Ray and delivered a demo tape of Steven's songs to Sparrow. Sparrow quickly set up a showcase for Steven. Both Bill Hearn and Peter York liked what they saw and made him a Sparrow artist.

Steven was extremely talented but there wasn't a ready-made market for his music. His first two albums didn't sell very well. When Billy Ray heard Steven perform during a Gospel Music Week showcase, he told Greg Nelson and Peter York, "You tell that guy to get away from the piano, pick up his guitar and never put it down again!" They delivered the message to Steven and that advice was a turning point in Steven's career.

However, Peter and Bill still had a tough decision to make. Because Steven's first two albums had sold less than 50,000 units combined, it was time to either let him go or double their commitment to Steven as an artist and go big on his third record. Thankfully for all of us they chose to go big. Steven's next album, ***More To This Life***, became his first best-seller when Christian radio began to embrace his single "I Will Be Here." A steady stream of number one songs soon followed.

Believing in an artist and overcoming every obstacle to help him or her succeed has been repeated many times in Contemporary Christian Music. My friend Chuck Fromm has often quoted a Bible verse that reveals a truth we frequently overlooked in our industry:

For not from the east nor from the west nor from the south
come promotion and lifting up.
But God is the Judge! He puts down one and lifts up another.

Psalms 75:6-7

It really is the Lord who promotes, and often despite our "professional wisdom." At the end of the day, all we could do was show up and make the best effort possible.

Chapter 21

COMIN' ON STRONG

One of the best things about finding success with major artists like Amy, Michael W. Smith, Sandi Patty and Petra was the cash flow they created. That supported our efforts with other artists who just needed an opportunity to be heard. The new CCM artists of the late 80's benefited greatly from the success those artists enjoyed. Just as Amy and Sandi had benefited from Evie's popularity years earlier, the process rolled on.

In the early days of CCM at Word, we weren't always the best at creating great albums but we were the best at selling them. And with a successful selling machine in place, we began to step it up in product development. Through the efforts of talented men like Gary Whitlock, Lynn Nichols and Neal Joseph, our artist roster got better and better, but our real muscle was always our distribution and marketing strength.

After Bob MacKenzie left Benson in 1984, the company went through a period of reorganization, merging Zondervan's Singspiration division (majoring in choral music) with its recording and music publishing operation in Nashville. Of course that meant some more personnel changes.

Wayne Erickson stayed on as President of Benson for a few months, but he was replaced in mid-1985 by Bill Traylor. Bill had been a part of the CCM explosion as head of the Impact label there in 1980. That meant he was well acquainted with Benson's most successful CCM artists: Dallas Holm, Tim Sheppard, Phil Johnson, Reba Rambo, Andrus Blackwood & Company, and of course, Sandi Patty.

Bill provided just the right A&R input for Benson at the time. He quickly signed Carman away from us at Word, re-signed DeGarmo and Key and took a real chance by signing a distribution deal that brought Benson a radical rock band from Southern California called Stryper. Of course, a few million record sales later, Stryper turned out to be a good decision.

THE CHAMPION

In 1981 Carman (born as *Carmen* Domenic Licciardello) released his first album through Buddy Huey's CBS Priority Records and was quickly invited to join the Bill Gaither Trio tour. Once again Gaither's platform helped launch a top CCM artist.

> **DID YOU KNOW?**
>
> **In 1994, Texas Stadium, former home of the Dallas Cowboys, hosted the largest Christian concert in history. More than 80,000 came to see Carman that night.**

After two records with Priority, Carman signed with Word in 1983. With the release of his first Myrrh album ***Comin' On Strong*** Carman became a high priority for our promotion department.

During Gospel Music Week in the spring of 1984, Word

was one of three labels to have its own night to showcase artists. Our choices for the evening were Leslie Phillips with her band, Michael W. Smith with his band, Carman with a guitar, and the number one rock band of all time, Petra, to close the evening.

▼ ONE OF CCM'S GREATEST PERFORMERS. Carman.
© CCMMagazine.com

That night as I sat in the crowd of 1,700 fans, retailers and radio executives at the Tennessee Performing Arts Center, I really thought we had set Carman up to fail. Leslie kicked the evening off and simply rocked the house. Then Smitty and his band threw every ounce of energy they had at their four-song set. Then it was time for Carman. No band. No background singers. Just Carman.

I noticed someone feeling his way along the back of the closed curtain, like he was trying to find an opening. And he was. Carman stuck his head through the curtain and smiled. The crowd laughed.

Then he emerged into the spotlight wearing a business suit and holding his acoustic guitar tightly to his chest. I dropped my head, *Oh no. We're in big trouble here.* And then Carman simply stole the show. His songs, his smile, his personality and talent just took over the room. After Carman left the stage, Petra never had a chance. He certainly was the champion of that night.

Although we did two very successful records with Carman, ***Comin' On Strong*** and ***The Champion***, he moved on to Benson in 1986. We didn't often lose artists to other companies. I suspect Bill Traylor made him a deal he couldn't refuse!

Bill did have a great ear for music talent and he had the good sense to promote great "sales talent" as well. After taking over at Benson, it didn't take Bill long to notice a very talented Singspiration field sales rep named Jerry Park. Soon Bill invited Jerry to Nashville to take over the Benson sales department.

Like Roland and me at Word, Jerry understood that a healthy sales and marketing team would be a magnet for artists. And when Bill Traylor decided to leave Benson in 1987, Jerry was the logical choice to replace him as president of the company.

A VIDEO REVOLUTION

At the time, the impact of MTV was exploding and Jerry realized that he had in Carman, the finest visual artist and entertainer in all of Contemporary Christian Music. Carman didn't always fit well on CCM airplay charts so there was only

▼ Stephen Yake and Carman discussing the script for a new video.
Courtesy of Stephen Yake

one way to push Carman to another level of sales—and that meant video.

Jerry (with a lot of encouragement from Carman) decided to invest a huge amount of money in a new Carman album and video project called ***Revival In The Land***. That investment paid off and in a big way. The album stayed at number one for 33 weeks on Billboard's CCM chart. It was truly a historic moment for Carman and for the entire CCM industry.

The Christian video revolution would soon catch up with MTV, and Stephen Yake played a large role in that launch. In the early 1980's, Stephen created a youth show called *Fire By Night* for Willie George Ministries in Tulsa, Oklahoma. Every show included Blaine Bartel's teaching and an interview with a top CCM artist like Benny Hester, Phil Keaggy or Second Chapter of Acts. It didn't take long for the success of *Fire By Night* to attract over 5,000 youth pastor subscriptions, and Stephen convinced Willie to add a produced music video to the program. Carman was the first.

Over the next few years, Stephen created amazing visual works for just about every major artist in the industry. His first Dove Award was for Michael W. Smith's "Secret Ambition." Many award-winning videos followed. His résumé grew to include work for Wayne Watson, Sandi Patty, Margaret Becker, Rick Cua, Kenny Marks and Petra.

JUST THE TRUTH

Jerry Park had taken over the helm at Benson during a difficult time for the company, but his sales and marketing expertise was exactly what was needed. In addition to Carman, Benson was home to Truth, the ultimate road-warrior group (approximately 300 concerts a year for a quarter-century).

MORE ABOUT...DICK & MEL TUNNEY

DICK AND MEL TUNNEY'S CCM ROOTS RUN DEEP. After touring with Truth for more than two years (1978-1980), Dick became The Imperials' keyboard player while Mel went to work in the Word Nashville office- all while they were building their songwriting catalogue.

While waiting in Word's lobby for an appointment in late 1982, Greg Nelson had the opportunity to hear one of Dick and Mel's latest tunes, "O Magnify the Lord." It didn't take Greg long to make that song a huge hit for Sandi Patty. And as her concert success soared, in 1986 she convinced Dick to become her musical director and invited Mel Tunney, Bonnie Kean and Marty McCall (then known as the group First Call) to join her on the road.

At the time, First Call had a blockbuster hit, "Undivided," and for the next 18 months they joined Sandi on one of the biggest tours in CCM history at the time, which included appearances on The Grammy Awards and NBC's *Johnny Carson Show*.

After he joined The Imperials, Dick and I played a lot of golf together and became very close friends. As most golfers have learned, when you spend four hours riding a golf cart together, sooner or later you will talk about something important. Dick was always there for me when I needed a friend, and I know he feels the same way.

Truth started in 1971 as an evangelistic outreach by Roger Breland, a young Baptist minister of music in Mobile, Alabama. The group became notorious for going any place at any time to sing and preach the gospel, and for giving platform to dozens of young singers, musicians and leading executives—many of whom would go on to become household names. The Truth alumni association includes Steve Green, Natalie Grant, Dann Huff, Neal Joseph, Dick and Melodie Tunney, Anthony Evans, Russ Lee, and several members of Avalon as well.

In the late 1980's, Truth also provided the launching pad for one of the most significant Contemporary Christian Music artists of all time, 4Him. Under Jerry's leadership, the A&R team at Benson sensed it was time for a new four-part CCM male group. While the 4Him guys – Andy Chrisman, Mark Harris, Marty Magehee and Kirk Sullivan – were still traveling with Truth, Roger Breland gave them the opportunity to sing a song or two as the group 4Him on Truth concert stages. Their first number one single, "Where There Is Faith," was showcased during those concerts.

▼ 4HIM - ANDY CHRISMAN, MARK HARRIS, MARTY MAGEHEE & KIRK SULLIVAN. © CCMMagazine.com

Jerry Park recalls hearing 4Him's new recording for Benson in the studio: "I just loved the sound of 4Him. We would go out of our way to the studio just to listen to those guys. I had never heard anything like that in the industry. They were the perfection of the Imperials."

Their first single exploded on the airwaves and rocketed up to the number one position on the charts. Just a few months later, 4Him won the Dove Award for New Artist of the Year *and* Group of the Year and that was just the beginning. Over the next decade, 4Him delivered three RIAA Gold Albums and a string of 27 number one singles.

Chapter 22

A NU THANG

By the mid 80's, it was clear that Word, Sparrow and Benson had emerged as the hub for our entire industry. We each had major artists under contract and growing distribution systems to attract the next wave of CCM talent.

Another not-so-obvious piece to the puzzle was also taking shape, thanks to the visionary insight from Dan Harrell and Mike Blanton. Mike had learned quickly during his time with us at Word. His primary insight was "that a large company like Word is more interested in selling great music, but not always focused on making great music." Mike and Dan knew how to find and make music that fans wanted. They had proven that over and over with their Blanton Harrell Management and the Reunion label.

Mike and Dan soon added another key piece to the puzzle that others would duplicate. They understood the value of a top CCM artist's platform. A highly successful Amy Grant created a touring opportunity for a new and upcoming Michael W. Smith. Then a highly successful Smitty would create a platform opportunity for the next great artist.

The combination of a great management team, quality music, and relentless touring propelled artists like Amy, Smitty, Sandi Patty, Steven Curtis, Carman and Petra to greater success. That helped Word, Benson and Sparrow to sell a lot of units.

Of course relentless touring required adding some new and very talented executives to make the process work. After observing the great job Malcolm Greenwood did promoting Amy Grant's ***Age to Age*** concert in Atlanta, Georgia in late 1983, Dan Harrell convinced Malcolm to join the team.

In a matter of days, he was in charge of Amy's ***Straight Ahead*** Tour that began in early 1984. The spring tour was a huge success thanks to promoters like Malcolm (who continued to promote her dates in the Southeast), Mike Bedford, Terry Garland and Steve Brallier, who handled the local promotion in markets across the country.

At the time, John Huie was a highly successful pop music agent in New York, and he and Malcolm had become friends over the last couple of years. Malcolm had no idea that John was about to fulfill his deep desire to help take CCM artists to the best and biggest concert venues in the country. The success of the spring ***Straight Ahead*** tour was overwhelming. As Malcolm planned the fall 1984 ***Straight Ahead*** tour, he realized that Amy and the promoters needed a new business model. He turned to his friend John Huie for advice. John not only gave wise counsel but he also helped book many of the dates for the fall tour.

Soon Amy and the rest of her team headed for a landmark tour of New Zealand and Australia. When they arrived back in the U.S., their first concert drew more than 7,000 fans at the Concord (California) Amphitheatre, thanks to John Huie—whom they had never even met.

As Amy and John were talking right before she took the

stage that night, John noticed a roar in the arena. "What is that?" Amy replied, "Oh, that's my piano player. He opens every show and the people just love him!" John quickly excused himself from the Amy meeting. He just had to see what that piano player was doing that the crowd liked so much.

Half an hour later, as Michael W. Smith walked offstage, he ran right into John Huie: "You don't know who I am, but I'm going be your booking agent." And 30 years later, he is still booking Smitty...and Amy. And Steven Curtis Chapman. All while helping build Creative Artist Agency in Nashville, one of the largest talent agencies in the world.

Of course Michael W. Smith wasn't the only CCM artist who benefited from being on Amy Grant's platform. Beginning in 1980, DeGarmo and Key's success grew immensely as the band opening for and backing Amy. As her popularity soared, D&K's record sales followed right along.

Eddie DeGarmo told me, "We really never did become a Gold or Platinum selling artist, but we were always good for a couple of hundred thousand sales on our albums." In other words, D&K's influence and reputation were larger than their album sales indicated. But in 1988, DeGarmo and Key had a far greater sales effect than even they could have imagined.

During a contract negotiation with Bill Traylor at Benson, Dan Brock, DeGarmo and Key's manager, made an unusual deal. As part of a new recording contract, Eddie, Dana, Dan Brock and their business partner, Ron Griffin, worked out a deal to form a new company that would handle all D&K international sales and publishing. Forefront Records was born.

Under the terms of their new deal, D&K would remain on the Benson label, and Forefront could sign other artists that Benson would distribute. Once again, a strong platform

▲ Forefront founders
Dan Brock, Dana Key, Eddie DeGarmo, & Ron Griffin
© Capitol Christian Music Group

artist (D&K) with great management (Dan Brock) would be connected to a top distribution system (Benson). But even Eddie and Dan Brock couldn't have imagined what would come next for Forefront.

JESUS FREAKS

Every major label had turned down DC Talk and The One Way Crew, but Forefront *was* looking for a rap group that could also sing. At a concert at Liberty University, Jeoffrey Benward (a new Forefront artist himself) said that from the stage. After the concert, a student gave him a copy of a demo cassette that Toby McKeehan had put together.

When Ron Griffin heard the tape he immediately called Dan Brock's house. Dan was in the shower, but Ron insisted that Darlene, Dan's wife, hand him the phone in the shower. As Ron played the tape over the phone, all three of them knew that DC Talk would be very big.

That deal opened the door for one of the most unusual CCM groups of all time—DC Talk and the One Way Crew. Toby McKeehan was "DC Talk" and Kevin Smith and Michael Tait were "The One Way Crew," but they always performed as a group. At the time, Toby was more of a rapper than a singer and "DC Talk" became shorthand for "decent Christian talk."

Eddie DeGarmo convinced the guys to shorten the name to DC Talk and they became the opening act for DeGarmo and Key. In 1989, as Eddie and Dan Brock stood behind the audience at Wheaton College at a DC Talk concert, they knew they had a huge hit group on their hands. As DC Talk finished their set, the crowd stood and chanted "DC Talk, DC Talk," over and over... and then they lined up at the merchandise tables to buy anything with DC Talk on it.

DC Talk began touring with D&K, and their audience grew rapidly. It didn't take long before DC Talk needed a larger platform, and Blanton and Harrell were more than happy to provide one.

Michael W. Smith's career was skyrocketing, and during his ***Place In This World*** tour, DC Talk was signed to be his opening act. That gave Toby, Kevin and Michael a platform in front of more than 10,000 new fans every night. Youth pastors brought busloads of young people out to every tour event. And DC Talk knocked it out of the park every time.

The tour was so successful that Michael invited DC Talk to join him the next year for his ***Change Your World*** Tour. DC Talk's ***Free At Last*** and ***Jesus Freak*** albums just flew off the shelves in stores and Forefront quickly became a force in the CCM industry.

Toby was a master showman. And at the 1994 Creation Festival (Tim Landis' event in Pennsylvania), he pulled off one of the most memorable moments in the history of CCM concerts. With 60,000 fans screaming "DC Talk," the group began their first song live—while entering the festival venue *in a helicopter*. The chopper landed behind stage as the group continued to rap and sing their way onto the main stage.

Soon after that, Billy Graham told his leadership team

Celebrating D.C. Talk's first Gold Record.
Greg Ham, Dan Brock, Danny McGuffey, Michael Tait, Jeff Moseley, Jeff Willett, Stan Moser, David West © Capitol Christian Music Group

that he wanted to invite Smitty and DC Talk to join him for their youth night events. His team balked but Billy would not yield. He said, "When I go to a foreign country, I use an interpreter. These guys are my interpreter to the youth."

So Smitty, Toby, Michael and Kevin joined Billy Graham at his first "Youth Night" event at Cleveland Municipal Stadium in front of a crowd of more than 70,000. Chaz Corzine, who was in charge of Smitty's tours at the time, remembers: "When Billy gave the invitation at the end of the event, the response was massive. Even outside the stadium people were getting saved. More than an hour after the end of the event, as we flew over the stadium, we could see thousands of people at the altar."

The same team took the stage at similar events night after night over the next few months. And the results were always the same.

Chapter 23

AND THE RACE IS ON

By the middle 1980's, CCM seemed to reach a tipping point. After so many years of very hard work, we saw a larger acceptance of the music on radio, TV and in churches and concerts. The hurdles we had all faced were falling away quickly.

CCM radio was booming with networks like KLOVE, WAY-FM and Northwestern leading the charge. All were growing dramatically and reaching into every corner of the United States. Even more traditional networks like Family Life Radio and Moody Radio were warming to the new sounds and adjusting their playlists. Along the way, radio pioneer Jon Rivers became the voice of the CCM Countdown program. The syndicated show was patterned after Casey Kasem's "Top 40" programming.

CCM artists were also making appearances on a vast array of Christian television programs on Trinity Broadcasting and Jim and Tammy Faye Bakker's PTL Network. The trail that Matt Crouch had blazed with his ***Real Videos*** show on TBN opened many doors. And thanks to Norm Mintle's tenacity, even the more conservative 700 Club began to feature our most high profile artists.

MORE ABOUT... JON RIVERS

Jon Rivers began his radio career in Jacksonville, Florida, shortly after returning from the Vietnam War. In 1985, he helped launch the original Christian format KLTY in Dallas. When KLTY temporarily moved away from Christian music just one year later, Jon began his work on countless Christian Music Specials with the top names in Christian Music. When KLTY re-launched its Christian format, he served as VP of Programming from early 1989 until August 2001, when he and wife, Sherry, joined the KLOVE Radio Network.

Jon has been heard around the world for over 40 years and his legendary show 20: The Countdown Magazine can be heard around the world on over 1000 outlets.

Christian music festivals began springing up all across the country and church buses filled with teenagers rolled through the gates. As more and more youth pastors bought into the ministry values of Contemporary Christian Music for their students, concert opportunities and attendance just exploded.

In 1978 Tim Landis pioneered one of the earliest Christian Festivals in Pennsylvania. "Creation Festival,"had become an annual event drawing more than 60,000 CCM fans every year. It was just one of many large regional events that became a central focus of our marketing efforts. And the church buses just kept coming.

Chuck Tilley, a successful advertising executive, attended a festival called Jesus Orlando in 1985. He was there simply to sell product, but as he watched dozens of teenagers give their lives to Christ that weekend, Chuck knew that it was time to do the same type of event in Atlanta, where he lived. He went home and met with his pastor, Dr. Paul Walker, at Mount Paran Assembly of God Church, and Mylon Lefevre, who was by that time also a leader at the church. After a few days of prayer they all felt a release to explore the idea.

AtlantaFest 1989 at the Atlanta Motor Speedway
© Atlanta Fest

So Chuck reached out to Tim Landis, Mike Blanton and Dan Harrell. Those four men produced the first AtlantaFest in the summer of 1987 at the Atlanta Raceway. During the first three years of AtlantaFest, they lost a lot of money and their partnership dissolved, but Chuck just couldn't give up.

He recalls, "That was what God told me to do." At the first festival alone more than 1,000 kids had given their lives to Christ. Young people were coming to AtlantaFest from all over the southeastern U.S. and many lives were being changed. Just two years later at AtlantaFest 1989, thousands of those young people would help introduce all of us to a very talented new Christian rock band.

FREE THE NEWSBOYS!

The Newsboys—seven young men from Australia—had a vision. They were going to America to do concerts and lead kids to Christ. Many would have called them naïve; no one in the United States had ever even heard of them. They weren't exactly a household name in Australia either.

In 1989, they landed at Los Angeles International Airport ready to fulfill their mission. Wes Campbell, who served as the manager and promoter of the group, remembers:

"The plan was really pretty simple. We grabbed our stuff off the plane and took a cab to a $25 per day motel close to Disneyland. We had enough money to stay there a few weeks and a whopping $2 per day per guy for food! We pushed two double beds together and somehow made it work. Two dollars per day bought a lot of cheap food at the 7-11, a block from our motel room.

"Armed with a recent CCM Magazine, my job was to call people and convince them to let us come and play at their events. Nobody was interested but I kept calling. Finally, the lady who was in charge of volunteers and staff at AtlantaFest asked her boss, Chuck Tilley, if there was any way we could play at the festival. He told her to tell us we could play for her group of workers late Wednesday night if we could get there."

The guys were ecstatic—they had a gig to play! Of course, they had no way to get to Atlanta, but they had six weeks to figure that out. As they "dined" at the 7-11, an older customer wandered over to the boys and asked what they were so excited about. They told him their good news. After a few minutes he approached them again, "I think the Lord just told me to give you my van. And why don't you come live in my basement and save your money for the big trip?"

Soon, the Newsboys discovered they needed tee shirts to sell at AtlantaFest. After telling their story to the owner of a tee shirt shop in LA, he printed their order for 1,000 shirts. Somehow he just knew that seven kids from Australia with no checking account and no credit card on file would be "good for the bill." He even packed the van for them as they left town.

The van guzzled oil all the way across the country and finally died—in the parking lot of Atlanta Speedway! The van was dead, but the Newsboys were very alive. After playing a late-night show on a side stage, the guys decided to sleep on the stage. The only other choice was sleeping in the broken-down van.

As they opened their eyes the next morning, they found themselves surrounded by teenagers waiting patiently to get their autographs. And many fans were asking when the Newsboys would play on the AtlantaFest main stage. That, of course, wasn't going to happen, so the kids started a petition to FREE THE NEWSBOYS! They collected more than 1,500 signatures.

Two days later, right before the star of the evening, Carman, took the stage, Chuck Tilley made the announcement, "We always listen to our customers. You want the Newsboys, you got the Newsboys!" The crowd went crazy, and at least one industry executive took note.

Weather kept some of the artists from getting to the event, so the Newsboys played six times at that AtlantaFest. In the process, they met Mylon and Broken Heart, who raised $1400 to put a new engine in their van.

They were soon off to Creation Festival for their next gig. Of course, no one at Creation even knew they were coming, but the Newsboys paid little attention to such details; they were moving in the grip of destiny. They found a way to play on a late-night side stage once again and made thousands of new fans…and sold $20,000 worth of tee shirts in the process!

After returning to Australia, the group realized that America was going to be home. In 1990, the Newsboys landed in LA again and became one of the most successful groups in CCM history. From a customer in a 7-11 store with a van to give, to a petition that put the Newsboys on the main stage, to a competing music group who loved them enough to fix that same van, the Newsboys demonstrated what it is to walk by faith and not by sight.

AtlantaFest went on to make history as well. In 1990, it moved to Six Flags Over Georgia, and over the next two decades, Chuck Tilley watched more than 20,000 teenagers give their lives to Christ.

Chapter 24
WHEREVER HE LEADS I'LL GO

Life is filled with incredible intersections that only God can create. Of course, it's always up to us to walk out every opportunity. And at the pinnacle of my career at Word in early 1985, I ran into one of those opportunities.

At the time, I couldn't imagine my life being any better. We had just launched the relationship with A&M Records. I still lived in my hometown surrounded by great friends made during my 15 years at Word. My favorite person in the whole world—my son Jackson—was just six months old. I was in charge of the largest Christian music company in the world, and I was spending more and more time learning God's Word and getting better at hearing God. Life was good, and I certainly wasn't ready to hear what He had to say next.

YOU WANT ME TO DO WHAT?

In May of 1985, we held our spring sales conference two hours south of Waco at the Lakeway Resort, just west of Austin. I loved going to Lakeway in the spring. There was plenty of golf, a great view of Lake Travis and another opportunity to beat Bill Gaither on the tennis court.

Roland Lundy had become our VP of Distribution. He and Dan Johnson, our VP of A&R and Marketing, took care of all the details, so my job at those meetings was really easy. I just showed up, made a speech at the dinner and enjoyed the recreation. What a deal.

I had hired most of the sales reps that came in from all over the country, and my relationships with our international distributors who were there was always good. It was a just a nice time away from the office with friends. Add in an appearance at this conference from Mylon LeFevre, who had become a trusted friend, and the week was sure to be a good one.

But for some reason I didn't enjoy the time. My spirit was restless, distracted, perhaps troubled. I finally decided to go back to Waco a day early. As I drove east on Ranch Road 620 toward Interstate 35, I asked the Lord about what I was feeling, and He made it clear—it was time to leave Word Records.

I was shocked, but He was emphatic, "Get out and get out now!" Thirteen days later I resigned. I had no idea what I would do next, but I had heard Him so clearly that I knew I was doing the right thing.

During the following few weeks, I spent a lot of time asking the Lord what He wanted me to do. After what seemed like an eternity, I heard Him again in my inner man: "Hang out your shingle and see who calls." Really, Lord?

So I rented an executive suite (you know, one of those offices that provides a receptionist and a phone line) and spent many days sitting at my new $500 desk reading and learning to use my personal computer. Soon I received three significant phone calls.

The first came from Bill Gaither. "I heard you left Word.

So, what are you going to do?" I told him that I honestly didn't know, but I suspected I was through with the Christian music industry. Bill just laughed, "No, you're not. And when you figure out what you want to do, call me. I want to be involved."

The second call came from Chuck Fromm at Maranatha!Music. He said, "I think I have the opportunity to buy Maranatha from Calvary Chapel. I want you to be one of my partners." Before long, I found myself negotiating the terms of that purchase with one of my faith heroes, Pastor Chuck Smith. By the way, that was a bit like negotiating with the Pope. Once the deal was done, I was one of four owners of Marantha!Music and took over the marketing and sales functions from my Waco office.

The third call came from Darrell Harris and Wayne Donowho at Star Song in Houston. Although we had sold a lot of Petra and Twila Paris records for them, they needed help. In

Darrell Harris, Twila Paris, Stan Moser, Jeff Moseley

other words, they needed some cash. So I bought 10% of the company stock and began helping them reorganize the company.

It didn't take long to realize that Star Song had great potential—and a lot of needs. Darrell knew how to make great music, and I knew how to market and sell great music. But to make all that happen we needed an investor. Without some serious cash infusion, Star Song just might go out of business.

I called Bill Gaither, "Bill, I guess I wasn't through with Christian music after all. I'm investing in this company called Star Song, and I wonder if you want to join me?" Bill sent his two right-hand guys, Jerry Weimer and Dan Lacy, to put a deal together. When they were through, Bill owned a third of Star Song, and his financial strength kept us alive.

Over the next three years, I invested every day in helping Maranatha and Star Song. It seems that I was on an airplane going to the Maranatha office in California or Houston (home of Star Song) or Nashville or Indiana nearly every week- all while trying to help raise my wonderful son, Jackson. Something had to give, and I sure wasn't going to choose work over my son.

MUSIC CITY, HERE WE COME

At Star Song, it seemed I was involved in one business crisis after another and at the same time caught up in the joy of marketing some of the best artists that CCM had to offer. I felt like the old vaudeville act of spinning plates. I kept running around the stage of my life, spinning the California (Maranatha) plate, then down to the Houston (Star Song) plate, up to the Indiana (Gaither headquarters) plate and finally over to the plate of Nashville (the growing hub of our industry). But I still lived in Waco.

By the end of 1987, I knew I couldn't continue running around the same track every day. I prayed diligently for several months and realized it was time to leave Maranatha!Music and focus on my role at Star Song. At the same time, the Lord made it clear that it was time to move to Nashville. He spoke very simply, "Go to Nashville and I'll meet you there."

Nashville just didn't make sense to me. Nothing in my portfolio said "Nashville." California, Houston or even Indiana would have made sense. Not Nashville—but He said, "Nashville." It was clear that if I moved anywhere else, I would be choosing to disobey.

Moving to Nashville and leaving Maranatha were equally traumatic. I was close friends with Chuck Fromm and my other partner at Maranatha, Tommy Coomes. It was difficult for them to accept the fact that I was leaving the company. They felt it was a broken promise and I did my best to understand their disappointment. I faced the fact that I could disappoint my partners and friends in California or I could disobey the Lord. So I stepped into the loneliness that often comes with following the Lord's direction in life. It was a very painful experience.

Leaving the familiarity of Waco and heading to Nashville was also a struggle. Our Waco house didn't sell for over two years, and my income from Star Song wasn't enough to cover the bills in Nashville. And frankly, Star Song was still in deep trouble. We had recently been forced to change the entire management structure and the company's future was clearly in doubt.

For a couple of years, I wondered if the Lord had made a mistake when He directed me to move. Or possibly I just hadn't heard Him correctly.

Nashville felt like a foreign country even though I had been there many times. Furthermore, my friends at Word and Maranatha!Music had become my competitors. In my heart, I really did believe that "God would meet me in Nashville," but honestly, I wondered why it was taking Him so long to find me. Life was a daily struggle but God really did have a plan.

At the end of 1988, six months after moving to Nashville, Darrell and Janet Harris, who were running Star Song down in Houston at the time, asked me to take the CEO role. I told them that I would, but that doing so would mean a lot of change; the company would have to move to Nashville. They agreed, and after months of deliberation they decided to stay with the company and join us in Nashville.

A new era for Star Song had begun, and the label would soon bring fans more Twila Paris, more Gaither Vocal Band, a new group called Phillips, Craig and Dean, Newsboys, and many other great CCM releases. We also became the distributor for Forefront Records and their DC Talk, Geoff Moore and the Distance, and Rebecca St. James records.

In hindsight, I can now see that when I drove down Ranch Road 620 on May 1, 1985, God knew exactly what He wanted to do with the next season of my life. It just took me a while to figure that out. And once again, without Bill Gaither's involvement and support, Contemporary Christian Music would have missed a great opportunity to reach those who desperately needed hope in their lives through our work at Star Song.

Change in life is often very difficult. But embracing change—sometimes radical change—is part of following Jesus. I made a lot of mistakes in the midst of some very painful and challenging times during those three years.

I had many of what Henry Blackaby, in his book "Experiencing God," calls "crises of belief." Did I really hear God? How can this decision be so painful for my friends and family? How will we survive? How did I get to this place in life? What will I do? All fair questions in the midst of the crisis.

You may be there in your own life today. None of us can possibly know all that God has in mind for our lives, but we can know He will direct our steps if we are willing to follow. When we see Him face to face, it will be too late to live by faith. Don't miss that opportunity right now. He is always taking us to the right place—if we will let Him.

Chapter 25

MY TURN NOW

My leaving Word seemed to accelerate the momentum there. My long-time best friend, Roland Lundy, took over the leadership, and Word moved into the next era of success. Very talented and experienced executives surrounded him.

Dan Johnson would soon leave to form his own company in Nashville. That meant Neal Joseph would lead the product development team. Loren Balman was more than ready to take the marketing team higher, and the sales department was in good hands with Tom Ramsey, who had been with us at Word since the early 70's. Although my departure was abrupt, the "A" team was all in place.

Right before resigning from Word, I finished negotiating a contract that brought Sandi Patty to Word Records. That *was* a big deal.

Neal Joseph's production of ***We Shall Behold Him*** had become Sandi's signature moment, but as we all now know, she was just getting started. After Neal left Benson for Word, Greg Nelson was their choice to produce Sandi's next record. Greg turned out to be the perfect choice.

Their first album together was called ***Lift Up The Lord***.

With Sandi's amazing talent, her sales continued to soar. Bill Traylor, Mike Cowart and the rest of the Benson team were ecstatic; but the best was yet to come.

For her next album, Greg decided to take a risk and produce ***More Than Wonderful*** entirely live in the studio. That meant singers, orchestra, rhythm section and Sandi all in one place at one time.

The musical dynamic Greg's decision created was spectacular, and honestly could not have happened without a brilliant vocalist like Sandi as the lead voice. When the recording sessions were done, Greg was amazed—all that music, all live, and they only had to re-record one line of one song.

More Than Wonderful flew to the top of the airplay and sales charts and became Album of the Year at the next Dove Awards. Four different songs from this one album ultimately won Dove Awards for Song of the Year!

This album not only launched Sandi to superstar status alongside Amy Grant, but it re-fueled Larnelle Harris' career. Greg just knew the chemistry between Larnelle and Sandi would be amazing, and he was right. He added Larnelle to the song "More Than Wonderful" and launched the most successful duet team in the history of Christian music.

Greg also produced Larnelle's next record, ***I've Just Seen Jesus***, in 1983 and the same duet formula produced another number one song and best-selling album. Those who saw Larnelle and Sandi perform together live will attest to the awesome combination that Greg Nelson brought to us all.

A few years later, Greg connected Sandi with another soon-to-be CCM legendary artist, Wayne Watson, to create ***Another Time Another Place***. That led to major television appearances for both Sandi and Wayne, including NBC's ***Tonight Show***.

Sandi's first album through Word was another classic produced by Greg Nelson called ***Morning Like This***. It hit the market in the fall of 1985. She received another Dove Award as Female Performer of the Year, but as big as ***Morning Like This*** was it paled in comparison to what happened next.

▲ SANDI PATTY SIGNS WITH WORD RECORDS.
Roland Lundy, John Helvering, Sandi, Dan Johnson
© CCMMagazine.com

STAR-SPANGLED BANNER

In 1986, Sandi Patty recorded "The Star-Spangled Banner" for a patriotic album. It was a very big production arranged by David Clydesdale, with additional verses written by Claire Cloninger.

Dan Johnson and his marketing team knew that the 100th anniversary of the Statue of Liberty celebration would be a perfect setup to take Sandi from well known "gospel singer" to national celebrity. So Dan attended a press conference hosted by the co-chairs, Lee Iacocca and filmmaker David Wolper. At the press conference, Wolper gave Dan the best path to pursue for the celebration's music.

So Dan relentlessly pitched Sandi's version of "The Star-Spangled Banner" as the song for the closing ceremony from the Statue of Liberty to be broadcast nationally on Sunday night, but ABC Television executives had never heard of her. After being turned down by Roone Arledge's team, he sent a cassette to Roger Goodman, who worked for Arledge.

Goodman decided to play the song on his way home from the office on the very Friday night that the Statue of Liberty celebration began; he immediately knew this was the right song for the show, and he quickly obtained approval from Roone Arledge to use it for the closing ceremony.

> **DID YOU KNOW?**
>
> **Sandi's appearance on ABC led to multiple television appearances including Christmas in Washington, Walt Disney's Fourth of July Extravaganza, and the 1998 Pepsi 400. She was asked to sing the national anthem at the Indianapolis 500 in 1987–88, 1990–92 and 2013.**

The only problem was that the ABC producers needed permission from Word Records to broadcast the track of Sandi's song. Of course, Dan was in New York attending the Statue of Liberty ceremony and could not be reached. So, Arledge's office did the only thing they could do on a Saturday morning. They called information in Waco, Texas, for a "Dan Johnson."

Dan's son Mark answered the phone. The voice asked if Dan Johnson was available. Mark answered, "No, Dan Johnson is not here. He's in New York this weekend." When the voice on the line explained what was needed, Mark confidently said,

"I can give you full authorization to use that song on your broadcast. No need to talk to anyone else."

Late Sunday evening, Dan got a call in New York from Roland Lundy talking about how great the television special was with Sandi's song closing the evening. Naturally Dan had no idea that had happened because he was at the ceremony, not watching it on television.

When he called the ABC Television office the next day, they told him the phones had been ringing off the hook asking about Sandi Patty. Before the end of that week, Sandi was sitting across the desk from Johnny Carson and then visiting the White House, all because one 17-year-old high school senior named Mark Johnson had given permission to ABC Television to air the song.

Amy, Smitty, Sandi, Mylon, Russ Taff and before long a new artist named Cindy Morgan led the sales charge at Word,

▼ Sandi Patty © CCMMagazine.com

along with a lot of ***Praise*** albums and ***Kids Praise*** albums developed by Maranatha!Music. Those were great days at Word Records.

My departure from Word certainly didn't hamper Sparrow's amazing growth either. Steve Green, Sheila Walsh, Margaret Becker, Michael Card and Whiteheart led the way. And Steven Curtis Chapman was about to have his own "Star-Spangled Banner" moment.

SADDLE UP YOUR HORSES

After "surviving the cut" at Sparrow with his second record, ***Real Life Conversations***, Steven Curtis Chapman realized he needed management help with his growing career.

▼ Singer, songwriter, performer, co-founder (with his wife, Mary Beth), of Show Hope adoption ministry, & a true friend to the entire CCM family.
Steven Curtis Chapman. © CCMMagazine.com

My former colleague, Dan Raines, had left the CCM industry a couple of years earlier to attend graduate school. His only music-related activity was serving as a board member and advisor to Michael Card.

Two years into that relationship, Michael approached Dan about managing his activities as an artist. Dan didn't really intend to get back into the music business, but that invitation from Michael stirred an old desire he had developed as an employee of the Los Angeles-based, Wayne Coombs Agency—the most successful artist management company of the 70's. So Dan formed Creative Trust in early 1988 with Michael Card as his first and only management client. His office was actually located on Michael's farm in Williamson County, Tennessee. In late 1989, Dan got a call from Steven Curtis Chapman.

Steven's third album with Sparrow, ***More To This Life***, was beginning to get noticed and he needed management help. While Dan loved what he saw in Steven's artistry and ministry, he knew the key to a breakout album would be a more strategic approach to touring. He called his friend John Huie. John had become a pivotal figure in the world of CCM concerts over the last few years, and Dan trusted John's instincts. As they spoke, Dan asked John to join him along with Steven and Mary Beth for lunch.

John Huie's impact on Contemporary Christian Music was already well known through his work with Amy Grant and Michael W. Smith. He had learned his trade very well during his days in New York as the hard-nosed lead agent for the top pop group The Police.

John arrived at Dan Raines' office just in time for lunch. As he, Dan and Mary Beth Chapman waited for Steven to make a pit stop, Mary Beth casually said, "I bet I know where

Steven will want to go for lunch." Mary Beth was 100% certain that she knew. "I bet I know which restaurant he will choose." Then she named the restaurant.

True to form, John didn't miss a beat, "Ok, you're on for $20. If he comes out of the men's room and picks that restaurant, I'm ready to pay up. In fact, here's my $20. Where's yours?" Now, Mary Beth wasn't normally one to make a real wager like that, but she was not about to back down. "Alright, you're on for $20!" John slid the two $20's into his pocket just for safekeeping. Of course, Steven picked another restaurant and John kept the two $20's without saying another word. Dan was freaking out inside and I'm sure Mary Beth and Steven wondered, *who is this guy?* They would soon find out.

▲ Steven Curtis Chapman accepting Dove Award.

© CCMMagazine.com

John Huie was and is a unique combination of "all business" and "all heart." Not only did he buy lunch, but John went "all in" with Steven Curtis and Mary Beth that day. Dan always maintained that was the best $20 she would ever invest in Steven's career, and he was right about that.

Sales of Steven's next new album, ***For The Sake Of The Call,*** grew steadily under Dan's management direction, but Steven's team was still looking for a "career defining" moment. Dan dropped by the studio as Steven was making his next album, ***The Great Adventure,*** and quickly knew what he heard was exactly what was needed to take SCC to a whole new level.

Shortly before the release date for ***The Great Adventure,*** John found himself on an airplane sitting next to Bill Hearn, who ran the label. It didn't take long for Bill and John to come up with a bold idea that would establish Steven Curtis Chapman as a major artist.

The Christian Booksellers Association's annual convention was set for Dallas just a few months down the road, and it was a huge promotional opportunity for all of our artists and authors. This gathering attracted more than 2,000 men and women who worked in the Christian retail industry; they came for seminars, showcase concerts and to order new products from all of us on the exhibition floor. Dan, John and Bill agreed: It was time to take a big risk and see just how far Steven Curtis Chapman could go.

They decided to create a Steven Curtis spectacular event at Reunion Arena during the CBA convention. The idea was to fill the arena with rabid fans *and* 2,300 attendees of CBA. There was no better way to show the Christian retail decision-makers how popular Steven had become. Booking an arena that held 11,000 people for an artist other than Amy, Smitty, Petra or Sandi Patty at that time was a huge risk, but the time was right. Steven Curtis Chapman was about to become, well, Steven Curtis Chapman!

The people did show up that night, including over 2,000 from the CBA convention. The show was a smash hit. As

Bill stood just offstage, the band kicked into Steven's new hit single, "The Great Adventure." Steven seemed to magically appear on stage with what became a defining lyric, "Saddle up your horses…" At that moment, over thousands of people rose to their feet and saddled up with Steven and Sparrow Records. It was done. Bill finally knew all the belief, hard work and risk they had taken with Steven Curtis Chapman was going to pay off. And it certainly did.

What Bill didn't know is that Steven almost missed his cue for that song. The concert had included 3 wardrobe changes, and Steven had one minute to make the last of those changes right before his big moment. As the band began the musical intro leading into "The Great Adventure," Dan Raines was in another part of the arena trying to help Steven with a wardrobe change.

Precious seconds ticked away as Dan helped Steven remove the tightest cowboy boots known to man. Steven was panicked. He just knew there was no way he would get to the stage in time. And Steven didn't know that the sound tech had turned his headset microphone on. The whole arena heard Steven tell Dan, "I'm not going to make it!" But like every other great performer, he did.

The horses *were* "saddled up" that night, and Steven Curtis Chapman's great adventure was in full swing from that moment on.

Chapter 26

OUR PLACE IN THIS WORLD

As Sandi, Amy, Smitty and Steven Curtis filled arenas night after night, our quest for "mainstream music" acceptance was fulfilled right before our eyes.

The A&M deal put Amy Grant and our entire industry in the spotlight. Amy's first pop single from the ***Unguarded*** album, "Find A Way," served as a good introduction to pop radio, but it wasn't the hit song we all had hoped for. However, Amy and A&M found another way to take her music to the masses with a little help from an old friend.

Michael Omartian, who had transformed The Imperials sound more than five years earlier, had continued to build his pop music career producing number one artists like Christopher Cross, Donna Summers, Rod Stewart and Kenny Loggins. A&M Records had also turned to him to produce Peter Cetera's second album, ***Solitude/Solitaire***.

Michael and Peter had just been handed a "sure thing" hit song, "Next Time I Fall" to record. It was written as a male/female duet. They both knew with the right female singer, it would soar to the top of the charts, but every big name female singer they wanted was locked into a recording deal that kept her from singing with Peter on his album.

So Michael mentioned Amy Grant to Peter. He scoffed, "Why would I want to work with a Christian singer that nobody knows?" During Amy's next trip to LA, Omar invited Amy and Mike Blanton to drop by the studio and meet Peter. It didn't take long for a recording date for "Next Time I Fall" to be set. Their duet soared up the charts to number one in the middle of 1986.

READY FOR PRIMETIME

Amy's success with "Find A Way" and "Next Time I Fall" proved once and for all that CCM artists were ready for primetime. Our decade-long dream of hearing our artists on pop radio had come true, and other general market record

BeBe & CeCe Winans
© CCMMagazine.com

labels were ready to take the plunge. While Amy and A&M were making hit pop singles, Sparrow Records began a venture into pop and R&B with BeBe and CeCe Winans.

The Winans had made a name for themselves as part of the PTL Singers. In 1984, they recorded a custom album for the PTL Network that included a Christianized version of the huge hit pop song, "Love Lift Us Up Where We Belong." Their version, "Lord Lift Us Up," became so popular that they were singing it almost every day while Jim and Tammy Faye Bakker ran the network.

By the summer of 1986, Sparrow Records was ready to take a chance on BeBe and CeCe. Billy Ray Hearn decided to match them with a producer named Keith Thomas (the same Keith Thomas who came to work for us at Word about five years earlier for $200 per week). Keith was just what BeBe and CeCe needed musically.

Sparrow had recently entered a distribution deal with Capitol Records' distribution arm (CEMA) to take its releases into general market stores like Target and Walmart. When Billy Ray and Bill Hearn heard the music Keith

MORE ABOUT... KEITH THOMAS

When Keith Thomas started working for us at Word in Nashville as a "song plugger" in 1982 for $200 per week, he was just a kid from Conyers, Georgia, trying to find his place in the CCM industry.

But he soon proved that sometimes a song plugger turns out to be a label president or even a top producer. Today, his producer credits include hit songs from BeBe and CeCe Winans and huge albums from Vanessa Williams, Amy Grant (*Baby Baby*), Michael Bolton, Carman and Selena.

Thomas created with BeBe and CeCe, they knew their self-titled record had more pop potential than Sparrow could deliver without some real help. So they turned to Capitol Records for that help.

Bill's first meeting with Jean Riggins (the product manager assigned to Sparrow) at the old Capitol headquarters on Vine Street in Hollywood didn't go well. Jean insisted that BeBe and CeCe Winans change their name, but Bill had a different plan. "No I really think BeBe and CeCe is so unique. In fact I think we should tone down the Winans part and use a big BeBe & CeCe logo." He was evidently right. Their first R&B (rhythm and blues) single from their self-titled album, ***I.O.U. Me*** hit the top of the radio charts, and their next two albums produced three more number one singles – "Always," "Addictive Love," and "I'll Take You There."

> **DID YOU KNOW?**
>
> During their career, BeBe and CeCe Winans have raked in several awards, including three Grammy Awards, nine Dove Awards, two NAACP Image awards, two Soul Train Music Awards and numerous Stellar Awards. They also have three Gold albums and one Platinum album.

JOHN LENNON, GUNS AND ROSES, AND MICHAEL W. SMITH

The Contemporary Christian Music that had faced so many barriers over the years was reaching the masses. All the early struggles with Christian radio stations, Christian retailers and even church leaders faded into the distant past. We had "found the music," and we really were positioned to deliver it to those who needed it.

Amy's success with Peter Cetera opened yet another door in late 1989. Mike Blanton and Dan Harrell got a visit from Ed Rosenblatt, who ran Geffen Records. Geffen was one of the hottest pop labels in the world at the time with artists like Donna Summer, John Lennon, Nirvana and Guns and Roses.

And Ed Rosenblatt just loved Amy Grant.

Of course, there was no way that Word and A&M would give up Amy, but Ed didn't come to the meeting just because of Amy. He wanted to distribute and promote Michael W. Smith (and a handful of other Reunion Records artists) through Geffen's marketing and distribution system. A deal was soon in place and the entire Reunion executive team went to Santa Barbara for Geffen's 10-year anniversary sales conference.

At the opening cocktail party for the event, Dan and Mike, along with Terry Hemmings, President of Reunion, and Melinda Scruggs, head of marketing, found themselves in some unusual company. Among the 600 Geffen sales representatives from around the world, one decided to make his feelings known about this upstart Christian label that "produced this weird music that had no business being part of their premiere rock label!"

"Are you with that Christian group?" he asked Blanton. When Mike answered "yes," the rep exploded with cursing and accusations about whether or not they belonged at Geffen. Clearly the battle lines were drawn. Dan Harrell had to break up the verbal assault, but the die was cast. Reunion Records had just stepped into the "real music business" grinder. As Mike left the room, he remembers saying, "God, get us out of here!" It's a good thing God didn't grant that request.

To make matters more interesting, just before Reunion was scheduled to make their big premiere presentation to the group the next morning, those 600 reps got to watch a video that included the Simpsons and Joni Mitchell promoting a movement called "Rock the Vote." The theme of that presentation was, "We need to get kids to register to vote because this Christian guy in Florida is trying to steal the votes of our kids!"

David Geffen followed that presentation with, "Now let's take a 15-minute break and we'll introduce our new Christian music label, Reunion Records." The Reunion team was on edge.

Fifteen minutes later, Melinda stepped to the podium and made a simple statement that turned the crowd around, "We don't know anything about the guy in Florida. We're here to make great music and sell records. So let's play some music!" She started with their new Ashley Cleveland record and the difficult moment turned into a standing ovation. The songs were all that mattered and the music was really that good.

Geffen Records never did have much success with Ashley's music but they sure did with Michael W. Smith. Just three years later, Smitty hit the number one spot on the Pop Music charts with "Place in This World" from his ***Go West Young Man*** album.

Geffen was always hopeful for pop success, but when your key artists are Guns and Roses and Nirvana, your pop radio promotion department doesn't always have a lot to do. During another sales meeting, their head of pop radio promotion, Clair Parr, heard "Place In This World" and volunteered to make it a hit. She did just that and soon followed up with another hit for Reunion, Kathy Troccoli's "Everything Changes."

Reunion's pop success was another breakthrough for our mission to reach the masses. First, Word with Amy Grant and Sandi Patty's Star-Spangled Banner moment. Then Sparrow Records with BeBe and CeCe. Then Reunion with Michael W. Smith and Kathy Troccoli. The barriers that had kept CCM artists isolated from the mainstream media were disappearing. Our success finally depended solely on our ability to find and make music that could compete on mainstream radio.

When Jarrell McCracken sold Word Records to ABC Television in 1974, he told us a big part of the reason was to use the world's cash along with its distribution and marketing systems to take Christian music to the masses. ABC invested millions to bring that vision to reality over the next few years. And ultimately ABC sold Word for a very handsome profit. The Christian music industry had become a good investment. And with every hit single, the secular music conglomerates' appetite for the profits that CCM could deliver grew stronger.

Chapter 27

A BRAND NEW START

When Darrell and Janet Harris asked me to become the CEO of Star Song at the end of 1988, we had no way of knowing the amazing opportunity in front of us or the obstacles we would have to overcome along the way. Darrell remained as president and head of A& R for the company, while his wife Janet continued to serve as VP of Operations, but our team was far from complete.

Darrell was one the best A&R men in the industry, but we needed a top marketing and sales executive at Star Song to match his skills. There was only one choice in my mind—Jeff Moseley. Somehow, I convinced Jeff to leave his leadership role at Reunion Records and join our new venture in Nashville.

My old friend Jackie Patillo moved to Nashville from California a year later, and she moved into a full-time position at Star Song. In time she became our VP of A&R. Hiring Vicki Dvoracek as our A&R Administrator completed that department.

Star Song was positioned for growth. Move the company—check. Hire the best marketing and sales guy I knew—check. Increase our A&R strength—check. And then thanks to our old friends at Word—Roland Lundy and Neal Joseph—our struggles began. Word signed Petra to a new four-album contract. In an instant, the group that produced 60% of the sales for our label was gone, just as I was taking the helm.

Two years earlier, Star Song had entered a new distribution deal with Sparrow. Because Sparrow needed our volume to expand their own sales force, it seemed like a good marriage of two independent, entrepreneurial companies. With our biggest-selling artist now signed with Word, I'm sure Billy Ray was re-thinking the decision to partner with us.

We did still have Twila Paris, Gaither Vocal Band and Steve and Annie Chapman under contract. All were successful artists but they didn't produce nearly enough sales volume to sustain the company. I knew that we were about to find out if we could stay in business long enough to release their next albums.

▲ Celebrating the new Imperials Star Song contract. Armond Morales, Dave Will, Jeff Moseley, and Stan Moser.
© Capitol Christian Music Group

We needed proven volume quickly. Jeff, Darrell and I reached out to some familiar names. Mylon LeFevre, The Imperials and David Meece had all lost favor at Word so we signed all three of them. We adopted a survival strategy on Petra; every time Word released a new Petra album, we released another "Best Of" album. Over the next few years, our 10 original Petra

MORE ABOUT...DANNY McGUFFEY

SHORTLY AFTER ATTENDING *BILLBOARD MAGAZINE*'S FIRST GOSPEL MUSIC CONFERENCE IN 1980, Danny McGuffey joined the Sparrow sales team. Just five years later he moved to California to become National Sales Director.

In 1991, he left Sparrow to become VP of Sales and Marketing for Reunion Records in Nashville. He helped make Michael W. Smith's "Place In This World" and Kathy Troccoli's "Everything Changes" major hit songs before joining Star Song in the same capacity in the summer of 1992.

At Star Song, Danny was a driving force behind the sales upsurge for Phillips, Craig, and Dean, Sierra and Twila Paris. He also created and implemented the strategy that delivered the Newsboys' first RIAA Gold record.

After Star Song sold to EMI, Danny began a 14-year career at Integrity Music that brought ***WoW Worship*** to more than 3,000,000 fans. He also developed ***Songs 4 Worship*** with Time Life that delivered 10,000,000 albums to U.S. customers and 1,000,000 more in Europe.

Danny has often described his work succinctly, "When God anoints a song it turns into a movement, and our job is to stand back and throw gas on the flame!" No one has fulfilled that mission better.

albums turned into 7 "Best Of" albums. That paid a lot of bills.

By the end of 1989, the Star Song ship was out of troubled waters. Our Sparrow/Star Song Distribution partnership had worked well for nearly three years, thanks to Billy Ray and Sparrow's Sales VP, Danny McGuffey. But it's very difficult for two very entrepreneurial and headstrong management teams to share anything. It would soon be time for Star Song to step out and start its own distribution organization.

WHITECROSS

Danny McGuffey was a great sales leader, and he liked our products...and us. So when he left Sparrow in 1990, Jeff and I hired him immediately as our VP of Sales. With Jeff Moseley's creative marketing and product development genius, Danny McGuffey's sales ability and tireless work ethic, and Darrell Harris' A&R excellence, Star Song began to grow rapidly.

We were doing well, but we still needed to replace Petra on our artist roster. Soon we identified the rock group Whitecross as the best candidate. Darrell and Jeff really liked their music and the marketing potential their lead guitar player, Rex Carroll, brought with the group.

We had to buy the label, Pure Metal Records, to get Whitecross, but it was worth the investment. Their first release sold 150,000 copies, but we still needed another breakthrough artist. And we found them asleep on the stage of AtlantaFest.

DID YOU KNOW?

In 2010, Heaven's Metal fanzine ranked Whitecross #4 on its Top 100 Christian metal albums of all time list.

NOT ASHAMED

Our radio promotion chief, Gayla Lowrimore, was there when the Newsboys took the stage at AtlantaFest 1989. Like the thousands of teenagers in the audience that night, she was blown away by what she saw. Upon returning to Nashville, she lobbied hard for Jeff and Darrell to take a look at this incredible group.

Just a month later, Gayla watched the Newsboys do the same thing at the Christian Artist Seminar in the Rockies, but this time many other label execs were in the audience as well. Gayla was convinced: Star Song just had to be the label for The Newsboys.

With Gayla's urging, Darrell Harris tried to call Wes Campbell. That wasn't easy in the world of no cell phones, and with a group traveling across the country in a van, but Darrell would not give up. Before long, the Newsboys came to Nash-

▼ NEWSBOYS © CCMMagazine.com

ville to perform a showcase concert for our Star Song team as well as other labels and producers.

In the end, Darrell and Jeff convinced them to sign with Star Song and we released their next two albums, ***Hell Is For Wimps*** and ***Boys Will Be Boys***. The combined sale of both albums was less than 20,000 units. Everyone was disappointed.

Record contracts at that time usually called for the label to exercise an "option" for each new recording. In other words, when we signed an artist to a contract for three albums, the contract really only committed us to record one album at a time. The label then had an option for the next album, and it was option time for Star Song and the Newsboys.

As we sat in our weekly A&R meeting, Vicki Dvoracek, our A&R administrator, announced that it was time to exercise our option to do another Newsboys record or move on. The cost to do that was contracted at $30,000. I quickly said, "Well, there's no way we're doing that one. Next!" Jeff Moseley, who was actually running the meeting, just sat there quietly.

I turned to him, "Jeff, you aren't seriously considering spending $30,000 on a record by that group, are you?" Jeff said, "No, but I think Darrell is; I've seen that look in his eyes before." I simply couldn't believe what I was hearing. Darrell wanted to do the record AND double the budget to $60,000! I looked at Jeff. "He's lost his mind. Would you please talk to him?" Darrell just wouldn't budge. He saw something in the Newsboys that record buyers hadn't heard yet. Darrell had the right to make that decision so I reluctantly agreed.

Darrell wanted our old friend and colleague Lynn Nichols to produce that album. Everyone liked the idea, but when Lynn couldn't take the job because of his work on a Phil Keaggy project, he recommended Steve Taylor (the "I Want To

Be A Clone" Steve Taylor) to produce. Darrell loved that idea and said he "knew God was smiling on us."

That new release, ***Not Ashamed***, sold 300,000 copies, but the best was yet to come. ***Going Public***, their next release, was even bigger. We had to make room on the wall for some more Gold and Platinum Albums. When I looked at those records on the wall I just shook my head. A group that I would have dropped without a second thought had quickly become a huge CCM success story. I guess that's why God made CEO's *and* A&R Chiefs.

HIS FAVORITE SONG OF ALL

While the Newsboys were beginning to soar, a solo artist named Randy Phillips, who wanted to record for Star Song, contacted Darrell. Darrell knew that at the time, the marketplace had more room for a group than for an individual artist.

As they discussed that, Randy remembered two guys,

▼ Phillips, Craig & Dean © CCMMagazine.com

Dan Dean and Shawn Craig, with whom he had sung at church meetings over the last few years. In a matter of weeks, they were in town performing a showcase concert for our Star Song A&R team. I was out of town, but Jeff, Darrell and Jackie thought the possibilities were worth pursuing. When we signed them to a low-budget contract, the new group – Phillips, Craig & Dean – was born.

Darrell put Jackie in charge of the recording, and they hired Paul Mills to produce. Jackie and Darrell picked the songs along with Jeff's help. That was easy; all three of the guys were very good songwriters. Jackie and Paul recorded the basic tracks and the guys flew into town to sing their vocals.

Most singing groups go to the studio after months or even years of singing together on the road. These artists had sung together very little prior to the recording sessions. They worked hard over the next few days, and with Paul's help the signature PC&D sound was birthed. The very first Phillips, Craig and Dean album was almost finished—but not quite ready for what would become a landmark first release.

> **DID YOU KNOW?**
>
> **Phillips, Craig and Dean have been juggling dual vocations as lead pastors and recording artists for more than two decades. They have created an impressive body of work inspired by what God is doing in their lives and their respective churches.**

As I walked through the lobby, there was no mistaking

the car sitting in front of the Star Song office. It belonged to a very well- known publishing representative, Dan Keen, who worked for Meadowgreen Music. His reputation as a great "song man" was well established and it wasn't all that unusual for him to be in our building.

Suddenly Jackie Patillo appeared in my doorway. "I need to talk to you and Jeff and Darrell about the PC&D record right now. There is a song you guys have to hear." I quickly explained to her that there was no budget left to record anything further. She wouldn't take no for an answer.

Jackie just knew. This song HAD to be on the first Phillips, Craig and Dean album. She played the demo for us and we were all amazed at what we heard. It didn't take us long to realize that "Turn Up The Radio" was a smash hit song. After all, what Christian radio station could possibly turn down the opportunity to play a song that promoted their very existence?

Jeff Moseley had even bigger plans than either Darrell, Jackie or I could imagine. While PC&D were recording their version of "Turn Up The Radio," Jeff had them record multiple versions of the song inserting the call letters of the top radio stations in America in the song itself. We had an instant radio hit on our hands.

"Turn Up The Radio" opened the door for a flood of great songs from Randy, Shawn and Dan, including "Favorite Song of All," which became the Gospel Music Association's Song of the Year from that same album. PC&D—three guys who sang together at church meetings from time to time—became one of the biggest-selling, most-played CCM groups of all.

I have often wondered if we would have ever heard "Crucified With Christ," "Mercy Came Running," and so many more PC&D classics if Jackie hadn't pushed us to record that song

Dan Kean brought to our office. That is the real story behind many artists and songs—someone in charge has to believe in the music before any audience has an opportunity to hear it.

A little over a year later, Jackie brought us the just-finished studio master of our second PC&D recording, ***Lifeline.*** By that time, the guys had sung together in concerts all across the country. As we listened to the playback, Darrell, Jeff and I all had the same question, "What did you do with PC&D?" They sounded too much like Benson's top-selling group 4Him. We quickly sent Jackie and Paul Mills back into the studio. We had to get the original "PC&D sound" back, and they did just that.

As Bill Gaither says, "A good song is written. And a great song is re-written." I'll add this as one who knows many stories like these,

"WITHOUT A GREAT A&R PERSON AND A PRODUCER WHO KNOWS HOW TO CRAFT THE MUSIC, THOSE GREAT SONGS JUST MAY HAVE NEVER BEEN HEARD."

Chapter 28

JUST SAY SO

While I was immersed in Star Song, my former colleagues at Word Records continued to build the largest Christian Music Company in the world in the Dallas area (the company moved from Waco to Irving, Texas in 1988). Roland Lundy was promoted to president of Word, Inc. in the process, and that opened the door for Neal Joseph to become the head of A&R and Marketing for all of Word's labels.

Neal would later found Warner Alliance Records, but not until under his leadership, Word's Label Group poured out hit songs from artists like First Call, Kenny Marks and Russ Taff. But possibly the best "signing" of that era for Word was adding John Mays to their A&R staff.

John had come into the industry as the bass player for the Speer Family in the late 1970's. So when Word needed a new A&R man for its Southern gospel quartet label, Canaan Records, John was a logical choice. Little did Neal know, but John would soon bring Word a very different kind of quartet.

John's first break in the CCM world soon came through a demo tape of a young girl who worked at a men's clothing

MORE ABOUT... WARNER ALLIANCE RECORDS

In late 1989, Neal Joseph, head of the Word Label Group, left the label to move back to Nashville and start Warner Music's new Christian label, Warner Alliance. His first artist was "Take 6," but the real breakthrough for Warner's new label came with Michael English.

Michael had been part of the Gaither Vocal Band for years. His first solo record with Warner Alliance in 1993 included the classic song, "Mary, Did You Know?" and soon-to-be GMA Song of the Year "In Christ Alone." The album sold nearly 200,000 units while earning Michael Dove Awards for Male Vocalist and New Artist of the Year.

His next album, *Hope*, was even bigger. With Michael's vocals and Brown Bannister's producing, *Hope* produced five number one singles and garnered multiple Dove Awards.

store at the Green Hills Mall in Nashville. At the time, her biggest glimpse of fame had been a demo version of "You Make Me Feel Like A Natural Woman" she had submitted to the hit television show "Star Search." But as only God could orchestrate, that demo led to an album that made her the Dove Awards' New Artist of the Year in 1988. That award was just the beginning of a string of hit albums for Cindy Morgan.

And yes, Cindy really did work at a clothing store. That's not uncommon for many who ultimately become well-known artists. In Nashville, many of those who serve the food or build the houses are songwriters and singers. It takes a lot of determination and sacrifice to fulfill a dream, even for the most talented musicians in the world.

Cindy's success gave John Mays a newfound freedom to look for the "next big Contemporary Christian Music female singer," and he certainly found one. Actually, he found four!

In the summer of 1992, John spent the week in Estes Park, Colorado, at the Christian Artist Seminar in the Rockies along with most of the leaders in the CCM industry. It was a great time to teach seminars, connect with other leaders and hear some very interesting, unsigned artists perform.

As John walked across the lawn of the YMCA Campground, an acquaintance emerged from one of the small artist showcase venues and said, "John, you've got to hear this group that is singing right now. I think their name is Say So; man, that girl can sure sing high."

John Mays was puzzled. The group Say So included his friends Jim and Kim Thomas from Nashville, but he knew Kim's voice very well. There was no way she was "singing high." So he stuck his head in the back of the room just to see.

Much to his surprise, he was watching another group named Say So, and his friend was right. These girls from Ouachita Baptist University could sing—high, low and everything in between. It didn't take long for John to do some song demos with them and invite the girls to join him at the Word offices in Nashville and talk contract.

Soon John made his pitch to the leadership team at Word in Dallas. "These girls can really sing. I know we can make hit records on them!" Loren Balman, who ran all of marketing for Word, remembers that meeting well: "Here were genuine, lovely, young women who had no idea what was really in front of them. It was clear to us all—let's make them a company priority and make this happen."

Loren and John Mays knew the first step was to connect this group of talented singers with a top-notch manager. Their choice was Mike Atkins. Mike's management company was already home to some of the most talented and acclaimed CCM artists of the day. Adding this new group to a team that already represented Petra, 4 Him and many others, opened the door with every concert promoter, magazine and radio station. If Word could deliver the right music, Mike and his team could help deliver the market.

The problem was the name. As John was finishing their first recording, what would become the premiere CCM girls group of all time was nameless. After months of trying, John, Loren, Mike Atkins and the entire Word Label Group marketing staff had simply not found the right name.

The name crisis was very real. They had one day to finish the album cover for their first album. It was so bad that at one point, John recalls, "We even considered calling them Sunflowers!"

Mike Atkins gathered the rest of the team and made it clear, "We have to keep meeting until we have a name." John sent 40-50 names to the group that next day, but he kept remembering a phrase from a C.S. Lewis book, "...we live our entire lives from a vantage point of grace." By the end of the day, four "genuine, lovely, young women" finally had a name. Point of Grace, the biggest-selling female vocal group in the history of Contemporary Christian Music was ready for takeoff.

BEFORE THEY WERE POINT OF GRACE, THEY WERE KNOWN AS SAY SO! Denise Jones, Shelley Breen, Heather Floyd, and Terry Jones. Courtesy Shelley Breen

Over the next few years, we would all learn their name very well. Their string of *27 straight* number one radio singles began with their very first song, "I'll Be Believing." As many of us in the industry often did, John Mays and Grant Hubbard, the head of radio promotion at Word, found themselves sitting by the fax machine at Word at midnight waiting for the radio charts to appear. That's just what you do when you are passionate about your work.

When their single was declared number one that night, the celebration began. And it continued 26 more times for Point of Grace, with songs like "Circle of Friends," "The Great Divide," and "Jesus Will Still Be There," leading the way.

▲ Up, up, and away! Launching the new Point of Grace album.
© Word Music Entertainment

The first two Point of Grace records produced by Rob Sterling sold very well, but when producers Michael Omartian, Scott Williamson, Phil Naish and Blair Masters delivered their third record, ***Life, Love, and Other Mysteries*** in 1996, the Word team was determined to make Point of Grace a Platinum selling group. Their strategy shocked us all.

By coincidence, the new Point of Grace record, ***Life, Love, and Other Mysteries*** was due to release at exactly the same time as Sparrow's new ***Signs of Life*** album from Steven Curtis Chapman. Roland, Loren and Mike Atkins, who managed Point of Grace, worked hard to get the upper hand. They were convinced they could sell 1,000,000 albums on Point of Grace and they were determined to launch that record like no other in the history of the Contemporary Christian Music industry. The plan was complex and very expensive.

Roland called his friend Norm Sonju, owner of the Dallas Mavericks, and arranged to charter the Mavericks jet for a day for a mere $53,000. Point of Grace, the Word marketing team, Mike Atkins and a lot of support staff soon found themselves on that jet preparing to deliver five private concerts—in *one day*!

The itinerary included Grand Rapids (home of Family Christian Stores), Chicago (headquarters for Moody Radio), Minneapolis (home to the Northwestern radio and store chain) and Oklahoma City, where the Mardel's store chain was located. The girls performed exclusive concerts for those key retailers and radio stations in each area and knocked it out of the park at every stop.

The cost was exorbitant, but ***Life, Love, and Other Mysteries*** did become Point of Grace's first platinum album. Clearly, the cost of the promotion was well worth the investment.

Chapter 29
LOOKS LIKE WE MADE IT

In 1971, I made my very first business trip for Word to Nashville. I know from personal experience that driving from Waco to Nashville in a 1970 Pontiac LeMans takes about 12 hours. I made that trip to Nashville more times than I can remember.

The roots of gospel music go deep in Music City, and that includes Contemporary Christian Music. As you have seen, just a few years after we formed Myrrh Records in Waco, Benson launched its own CCM label Greentree Records in 1976 in Nashville. Reunion Records came to life there in 1983, and Forefront joined the party in 1988, just one year before Star Song made the move to Nashville from Houston. Nashville was rapidly becoming "*Contemporary Christian Music* City."

TENNESSEE WALTZ

At Sparrow, Billy Ray Hearn was dealing with two realities that would make Sparrow the next company to make the move. In 1986, Peter York, his head of A&R for the label, had convinced Billy Ray to move him to Nashville and open a Sparrow Records office on Music Row. It just made sense—most of their roster of artists and writers lived there.

The other reality was the cost of doing business in California. When Sparrow outgrew their Chatsworth, California, shipping facility in 1989, Billy Ray made a very wise investment—he decided to build a warehouse and fulfillment center for Sparrow in Illinois right next to Capitol Records' distribution facility. That decision saved Sparrow an enormous amount of overhead and allowed its customers to receive shipments much faster. Ultimately, that decision made a move to Nashville possible.

The Sparrow artist roster continued to grow through Peter York's presence in Nashville. It didn't take long for Peter to push Billy Ray to move the entire company there. Sparrow closed its Chatsworth, California office on a Thursday afternoon in early 1991, and on Monday morning, 57 families had been moved to Music City where the company was open for business.

Moving the company was just the first step in a five-year chain of events that transitioned Sparrow from its role as a California-based independent record label to the leading company in all of the Christian music industry, but it took a gut-wrenching decision to make that happen. By the end of 1991, Billy Ray had to make that decision—Capitol Records was determined to buy Sparrow.

Jimmy Bowen was the head of Capitol Records (a division of EMI) in Nashville at the time. After reviving both Polygram and MCA Records in Nashville, Bowen (as he liked to be called) found great success at Capitol with a new artist named Garth Brooks. Jim Fogglesong had originally signed Garth, but when Bowen replaced Jim, he focused the entire company's

Jimmy Bowen, Billy Ray Hearn, and Jim Fifield complete EMI's purchase of Sparrow Records.
© Capitol Christian Music Group

attention on making Garth the star that he became.

In the midst of that success, Bowen came to Billy Ray with a clear vision, "Christian music is going to be as big as country music, and I want to be a part of that." And he was willing to put all the muscle of Capitol Records behind that vision.

The idea of selling Sparrow didn't sit well with Billy Ray at first, but Bowen insisted they both go to New York to meet with his boss, Jim Fifield, the head of Capitol/EMI worldwide. Before making the trip, Billy Ray sought the counsel of his most trusted advisors: Buck Herring (Second Chapter of Acts), Pastor Jack Hayford (Church on the Way), New Zealand author Winkie Pratney and Pastor Jim Cymbala (Brooklyn Tabernacle). Three of them said "No." But Jim Cymbala answered Billy Ray's question with a question of his own, "Your purpose has always been to get the message of Christ out. Will they help you do that?"

After meeting with Fifield and Bowen in New York, Billy Ray knew what to do. It was time to make a deal. In early 1992, Sparrow became part of Capitol Records Nashville.

In early 1992, Sparrow became part of Capitol Records Nashville.

TOGETHER AGAIN

At Star Song our sales just kept soaring. The void in the market that was created by Amy Grant's moving more toward pop music created more room for Twila Paris in CCM radio; her single "God Is In Control" flew to the top of the charts.

After our Sparrow Star Song distribution agreement ended in late 1990, we quickly built our own distribution team. In early 1992, Forefront Records was ready to find a new distribution partner and Star Song was the perfect choice.

Dan Brock had been a Star Song fan since his days as Petra's manager. He was sold on Jeff Moseley's and Danny McGuffey's ability to deliver great marketing and distribution plans. We quickly entered a distribution arrangement with Forefront Records that brought us DC Talk, Geoff Moore and the Distance, and Rebecca St. James.

Our Newsboys story continued to grow

DID YOU KNOW?

At Word, Loren Balman poured himself into the creative and business challenges surrounding his vision for *My Utmost For His Highest*. The text from Oswald Chamber's daily devotional book inspired Loren so much that he was determined to help craft songs for an album that would reach believers and nonbelievers alike.

In Loren's mind, he was "creating a soundtrack for life." It took many hours of negotiation, but *My Utmost For His Highest* became a reality and featured Steven Curtis Chapman, 4 Him, Amy Grant, Twila Paris, Phillips, Craig and Dean, Sandi Patty, Michael W Smith, Point of Grace, Bryan as well. Every album became certified gold or platinum for sales exceeding 1,000,000 units. And through our relationship with the Gaither Vocal Band we launched the famous "Homecoming" series of DVDs and CDs.

In just five years, annual sales at Star Song had grown from $4,000,000 to over $32,000,000. That made Star Song a prime acquisition target for Jimmy Bowen. In October 1994 the sale of Star Song to Capitol/EMI was finalized, and Star Song was reunited with Sparrow once again. The EMI Christian Music Group would quickly become the largest Christian music company in the world.

MUSIC CITY HERE THEY COME

At the time, Word was still located in Irving, Texas, but in 1993, they joined the rest of us in Nashville as a newly acquired part of Nashville's Thomas Nelson publishing company. Nelson had tried to acquire Star Song for a couple of years but we never saw our company culture as a fit with Thomas Nelson. In hindsight we made the right choice.

The merger of Sparrow and Star Song, along with EMI's marketing and distribution resources, made the newly formed EMI Christian Music Group a serious competitor for Word's three-decade position as the largest company in the industry, but Word wasn't going to take a backseat easily. Their success continued with artists like Sixpence None The Richer, Anointed, more Sandi

▲ Billy Ray Hearn and the Sparrow team in 1995.

Patty, Jaci Velasquez, Burlap to Cashmere, the best-selling collection entitled ***My Utmost For His Highest***, and through their distribution arrangements with Toby Mac's Gotee Records and Michael W. Smith's Rocketown Records.

Over at the Benson Company, Jerry Park and his top marketing executive, Allan Hardin, enjoyed huge success with 4 Him, Carman and Stryper. Little did they know that the biggest commercial radio single in the history of Contemporary Christian Music would emerge from an unlikely artist just a couple of years later.

In 1992, the Benson Company had been sold to a pop music executive named Wes Farrell. After Wes' death in 1996, Benson ended up in the hands of Clive Calder's Zomba Music Group. Zomba had acquired Brentwood Music from Jim Van Hook in early 1994 as well. Jim, having been a key executive at Benson years earlier, urged Clive to buy Benson. The amazing story of radio success with "Butterfly Kisses" was about to unfold.

OPRAH AND THE BUTTERFLY

Jeff Moseley became the president of The Benson Company in early 1997. By then, Bob Carlisle's song, "Butterfly Kisses," had already been to the top of the CCM radio charts as part of Bob's 1996 album, ***Shades of Grace***, but none of us could have anticipated what happened next.

Clive Calder's wife, Patricia, soon heard "Butterfly Kisses" and became a fan of the song. It didn't take long for Jeff and Clive to develop a strategy to take it to pop radio. And radio agreed with Patricia. "Butterfly Kisses" was played relentlessly.

After reaching the number one spot on pop radio charts across the country, Bob Carlisle sat on the couch next to

Oprah Winfrey the week of Father's Day 1997. He had just sung "Butterfly Kisses" for her adoring fans, and Oprah had become a fan. During the next week, Bob's album, which Jeff had re-titled as ***Butterfly Kisses***, sold more than 250,000 units—an all-time sales record for a CCM album.

DID YOU KNOW?

"Butterfly Kisses" was written for Bob Carlisle's daughter Brooke's 16th birthday. The song came to him while he was going through old photos in his office and realizing she'd be leaving home soon. The album ultimately qualified for RIAA double platinum status for more than 2,000,000 units sold.

Naturally, that was the crowning moment of Bob Carlisle's career. It also marked a major "finish line" for all of us who had worked so hard to deliver Contemporary Christian Music to the masses. For 30 years, we had cleared every hurdle along the way. From church leaders who just knew that drums and guitars were evil, to Christian radio networks and retailers who weren't quite ready for CCM, to pop radio success, the race had been filled with challenges.

It had been 30 years since the first rumblings of what would become Contemporary Christian Music. Thirty years of working to penetrate American culture with music that impacted so many lives. And as Oprah looked in the camera and told America about one of our own, we had arrived.

Our music really was good enough for prime time. Amy, Smitty, Steven Curtis, Sandi, BeBe and CeCe and now Bob Carlisle had reached the summit we had only seen from a distance. Contemporary Christian Music was no longer hidden on a small shelf in a remote mom-and-pop bookstore. By the grace of God, we had succeeded beyond what any of us could have possibly imagined.

Epilogue

I CAN SEE CLEARLY NOW

My years at Star Song were some of the best of my life. We were truly a team that only God could have brought together. In just five short years, we took a company that employed 12 people in Houston, Texas, to a team of 82 dedicated people in Nashville who helped bring Twila Paris, Gaither Vocal Band, Phillips, Craig and Dean, Newsboys, DC Talk and so many other great artists to fans.

However, as much as I enjoyed my Star Song years, there really is no place like home. I often look back on my 15 years at Word Records with real amazement. In spite of our faults and failures, God really did use a bunch of ordinary people to bring clear and strong Christian songs to the nation and around the world.

After we sold Star Song to EMI, I realized that I had reached another turning point in my life. Three months after closing the sale, my new boss, Jimmy Bowen, was diagnosed with thyroid cancer. Bowen knew it was time for him to step aside, and that changed everything. Before long I had another new boss and I didn't like the career path that he had in mind for me at the EMI Christian Music Group. I soon stepped aside from nearly 25 years in leadership.

As I look back over the decades, I am very grateful for the lasting relationships that were built during that 25-year career. And after writing this book, **I now understand what Amy Grant was trying to say three decades ago in the A&M recording studios,**

"THE BEST PART OF ALL THIS IS THAT WE'VE ALL BEEN TOGETHER AS FRIENDS FROM THE VERY BEGINNING..."

Whether the people you have read about here were my colleagues or competitors along the way, we really did stand together to deliver hope to many who needed to hear. We stood hand in hand, investing our lives and often our fortunes, to make a living and have an impact on listeners around the world, and the friendships that we discovered along the way are still very much alive.

Many of us have also stood hand in hand to deliver this book—the real story behind the artists, songs and executives who built the Contemporary Christian Music industry—to you.

If you run into any of those fine people listed on pg. 233 take a moment and thank them. Thank them for believing in the songs that have impacted your life. And thank them for helping me tell this story—this amazing story of how God turned our own struggles and shortcomings into a living testimony of His goodness and grace.

THAT IS ALWAYS A STORY WORTH TELLING.

THANK YOU...

I will always be amazed and grateful that God chose to place me in the midst of so many talented and dedicated singers, songwriters, and executives over the last four decades. There is simply no way a book like this could be written without His relentless grace and the passionate, and sacrificial efforts of dozens of those colleagues and friends who lived this story with me.

WORDS COULD NEVER EXPRESS HOW GRATEFUL I AM FOR MY WIFE, SUE MOSER. Thank you for being there, day after day, story after story, and edit after edit of this writing adventure. God has blessed me exceedingly and abundantly beyond all I could ask or imagine—through you.

THANK YOU ED CHINN. Your wisdom, counsel, wonderful editing talents, and friendship over so many years has enriched my life and now the lives of those who read this amazing story.

THANK YOU BEVERLY WALLBRECH. Your amazing artistic talent is a true gift. And the personal belief that you and your husband, Ian, have shown me over the last few years has been a cornerstone of every writing effort.

THANK YOU DANNY MCGUFFEY. Your immediate support and encouragement when this book was just a dream has sustained me throughout the entire process. I look forward to all God wants to do through you in the days ahead.

And…

THANK YOU TO ALL THOSE LISTED BELOW WHO LIVED THIS AMAZING STORY OF GOD'S GRACE AND WERE WILLING TO SHARE YOUR STORY AND YOUR HEART WITH THOSE WHO WILL READ THESE WORDS. I'M GRATEFUL FOR THE FRIENDSHIP THAT GOD HAS GIVEN US.

ALLAN HARDIN
ALLEN WEED
BILL GAITHER
BILL HEARN
BILL TRAYLOR
BILLY RAY HEARN
BRENDA BOSWELL
BROWN BANNISTER
CARMAN
CHARLES DORRIS
CHAZ CORZINE
CHRIS CHRISTIAN
CHUCK FROMM
CHUCK TILLEY
CRICKET SEHR
DAN BROCK
DAN HARRELL
DAN JOHNSON
DAN POSTHUMA
DAN RAINES
DANNY MCGUFFEY
DARRELL HARRIS
DAVID BREEN
DAVID PIERCE
DAVID SMALLBONE
DICK TUNNEY
DON FRANCISCO
EDDIE DEGARMO
ELWYN RAYMER
FRANK EDMONDSON
GIL FEW
GREG HAM
GREG NELSON
JACKIE PATILLO
JEFF MOSELEY
JERRY PARK
JOE BATTAGLIA
JOEY ELWOOD
JOHN HUIE
JOHN MAYS
JOHN STYLL
KENT SONGER
KURT KAISER
KYLE FENTON
LLOYD PARKER
LOREN BALMAN
MALCOLM GREENWOOD
MATT CROUCH
MELODIE TUNNEY
MICHAEL BLANTON
MICHAEL OMARTIAN
MIKE ATKINS
MIKE COLEMAN
NEAL JOSEPH
NORM MINTLE
PETER YORK
RALPH CARMICHAEL
RANDY MOORE
ROD RILEY
ROLAND LUNDY
RONN HUFF
STAN MOORE
STEPHEN YAKE
TERRY HEMMINGS
TIM LANDIS
WES CAMPBELL